the WATCHMAN

the WATCHMAN

SEER AND PROPHET, ISSACHAR AND MESSIAH
PUT TOGETHER IN ONE SOUL TO FORM THE SPIRIT OF PROPHECY ON EARTH

EMMANUEL NUHU KURE

Carpenter's Son Publishing

Printed in the United States of America
By **Carpenter's Son Publishing,** Franklin, TN
In association with Larry Carpenter
Christian Book Services, LLC

www.christianbookservives.com

ISBN: 978-1-952025-43-3

Forward All Inquiries to:
The Vision Pioneer's Office
Throneroom (Trust) Ministry
ZION International Prayer and Retreat Camp
Throneroom Close, Off Hospital Road
PO Box 266, Kafanchan, Kaduna State, Nigeria
E-mail: ttmvisionpioneeroffice@gmail.com
www.throneroomtrustministry.org
+234 805 1817 164

USA
1114 Bella Vida Blvd, Orlando, FL 32828
+1 850 5590 024

TABLE OF CONTENT

PART 1

DEDICATION

To the Bright and Morning Star – Yeshua Hamashiach is this book dedicated, to serve the purpose of His coming and to release His chosen generation.

APPRECIATION

Thanks to Dr. Steve Ogan a foremost "Issachar" spirit man for writing the forward to this sensitive book.

To Pat Francis, God's vessel of honor for her prophetic word to light up the path of the Saints, "thank you."

Glory to God for Bill and Judy Combs who facilitated the printing in the US and contributed to its production. And lastly, thanks to Kim Sunday Jacob, my office Administrator, for sleepless nights to see that this book is published.

The Lord remember you all.

THE WATCHMAN, Apostle Emmanuel Nuhu Kure.

Hearts are crying out for you! Nations are waiting for you! For the earnest expectation of the creation eagerly waits for the revealing of the sons of God. (Rom. 8:19). You are a Watchman, son, and daughter of God, for such a time as this! This book is a must-read that will help you to discover your Watchman Anointing of the powerful great glory of Christ in you. You are the Voice of the Lord on earth. As God's Watchman, God has given you authority to enforce God's Kingdom and Will on earth as it is in heaven. Like a Shofar the voice of the Lord, through you demonic forces shall be destroyed and forced to set people, communities, and nations free. The voice of the Lord through you will manifest His Glory in miracles, signs, and wonders. The voice of the Lord through you will declare times and seasons. The voice of the Lord through you will call things that are not to a reality. This book will inspire you, motivate you, and train you in your Watchman Glory.

Dr. Pat Francis
Toronto, Canada

FOREWORD

A tide has turned. A seal is broken and the sights and sounds from the Lamb's altar in Heaven must be seen and heard by the watchmen on earth. These are the ones who can hear the trumpet sound and compel nations to take heed of the last day warnings of the Lord.

In *The Watchman,* Prophet Emmanuel Nuhu Kure unveils the prophetic picture of the original Watchman as celestial prototypes of seers and prophets called to fulfill the Issachar Mandate of the Messiah. He paints a vivid picture of the Celestial Watchman as watchers and holy ones. He gives us deep insights into their profile as "Keepers of the field," instruments of fulfilling Messianic prophecies, agents of establishing and enforcing God's statutes, and harbingers of times and seasons of divine visitation.

From the profile, Kure inspires the redeemed watchmen to function as shofars of God anointed to proclaim the Lordship of the Messiah and open the spiritual highways of nations to pave the way for the hosts of Heaven. He deepens our perception of how to confront and conquer those who rouse Leviathan, the proper dimensions of understanding prophetic prayers and actions against the Zanzummims or sworn enemies of God, and how to possess the gates and keep the watches.

This book is full of testimonies of the power of the watchman in Jerusalem, the United States of America, the Caribbean, and on the Continent of Africa. It is a prophetic guide for all those who understand that an end-time seal has been broken for the ultimate battle of the last days to commence. It is precise, practical, and therefore well-written. I consider *The Watchman* a compulsory reading for all leaders on whose shoulders lie the Issachar mandate of understanding the times and knowing what to do.

Dr. Steve OGAN
Port-Harcourt, Nigeria

PREFACE

Times have changed. Jesus Christ is creating new voices for Himself. Voices that will move at the same pace with His wheel in Ezekiel Chapter One. Voices who rise when He rises and settle when He settles. Oracles who will not live for themselves but Him alone. Broken vessels who have no will of their own but His own alone.

The Corona Virus that conquered the world and stopped time and reset the clock of the earth both in the spirit and in the physical has seen to this. The virus marks the removal of the veil for a new revelation. It has ushered in the season of the Messiah, and all those who work for Him both in the spirit and the physical. It has opened the veil for both Angels and men to work together. The era of the reign of the watchmen has begun. "Thy will be done on earth as it is in heaven has begun." Martyrs will be born that new heavens may be set.

Sacrificial lambs who live only at the instance of God will begin to dominate both the political and spiritual earth. This first part of the book on the Watchman will be the opening of the gates.

May the Spirit of God birth you in your real form and your new and permanent glory. That you may fulfill the purpose for which you were born as a Watchman.

"And the Angel took the censer, and filled it with fire of the altar, and cast it into the earth: and there were voices, and thundering, and lightning, and an earthquake. And the seven angels which had the seven trumpets prepared themselves to sound." (Revelations 8:5-6)

Let the other sounds begin in all the earth from now henceforth till the coming of Yeshua Hamashiach.

Apostle Dr. Emmanuel Nuhu Kure
12th September, 2020. 23rd Elul, 5780

Ezekiel 33:1-9

" *Again the word of the Lord came unto me, saying, Son of man, speak to the children of thy people, and say unto them, when I bring the sword upon a land, if the people of the land take a man of their coasts, and set him for their watchman: If when he seeth the sword come upon the land, he blow the trumpet, and warn the people;*

Then whosoever heareth the sound of the trumpet, and taketh not warning; if the sword come, and take him away, his blood shall be upon his own head. He heard the sound of the trumpet, and took not warning; his blood shall be upon him. But he that taketh warning shall deliver his soul. But if the watchman see the sword come, and The Watchman *blow not the trumpet, and the people be not warned; if the sword come, and take any person from among them, he is taken away in his iniquity; but his blood will I require at the watchman's hand.*

So thou, O son of man, I have set thee a watchman unto the house of Israel; therefore thou shalt hear the word at my mouth and warn them from me. When I say unto the wicked, O wicked man, thou shalt surely die; if thou dost not speak to warn the wicked from his way, that wicked man shall die in his iniquity; but his blood will I require at thine hand.

Nevertheless, if thou warn the wicked of his way to turn from it; if he do not turn from his way, he shall die in his iniquity; but thou hast delivered thy soul. "

1

THE WATCHMAN

It all began in Heaven the dwelling place of God. The Watchman has always been part of the divine order. The "Let Us" first. The Thrones of God. The Twenty-four Elders with Crowns. The Angels in their different formations and ranks and assignment. All creatures of the "Let US" or He that was later to be known as Hashem – God Almighty. Heavenly creations and later earthly creations. Among these great constellations and divinity, a set of Angels were the keepers of time. The mainstream of which was known as Watchers and Holy Ones in scripture led by the Arch-Angel of Prophecy or Time – Gabriel.

The Watchman is therefore a version of the heavenly messengers and the Holy Ones on earth.

Daniel 4:13, 17 and 23 says,

> *"I saw in the visions of my head upon my bed, and, behold, a watcher and an holy one came down from heaven; his matter is by the decree of the watchers, and the demand by the word of the holy ones: to the intent that the living may know that the Most High ruleth in the kingdom of men, and giveth it to whomsoever he will, and setteth up over it the basest of men. And whereas the king saw a watcher and an holy one coming down from heaven, and saying, Hew the tree down, and destroy it; yet leave the stump of the roots thereof in the earth, even with a band of iron and brass, in the tender grass of the field; and let it be wet with the dew of heaven, and let his portion be with the beasts of the field, till seven times pass over him."*

Most functions carried out by watchers in the heavenly places are the same function that watchmen and intercessors do on earth. The watchman is the "Keeper of the Field" (Genesis 2:15). He watches after things that God has created. He has authority and power over every creature and sustains what God has created.

WATCHERS AND
HOLY ONES

Watchers are Angels, who fulfill Messianic prophecy at the appointed time. They announce and move things into place according to the will of God when their time of fulfillment has come. They serve only one God. It is written in the Holy Scriptures that "the TESTIMONY of Jesus is the Spirit of Prophecy." Prophecy is the ordained or appointed time for events to take place. Watchers bring prophecy to reality and put events together as the CREATOR wants it.

The Angel attached to Moses was a watcher. The Lord told Moses that the work of the Angel was to bring him through the wilderness and that the Angel would not respect his person or do his bidding but only the bidding of the One that sent him. If Moses had gone against God's word, the same Angel that was sent to protect him would have destroyed him.

The watcher, likewise, connects you to your destiny as you remain faithful and focused on the One that sent him. The watcher only obeys the words and desires of God. He sometimes stands in the authority of the Master to carry out his functions. The watchman maintains his emotions and his love for God that triggers his constant worship of God. He has never lost his servanthood and loyalty to God despite his emotions which have been redeemed or tamed by his knowledge of Christ.

THE MESSIANIC SYMBOL OF MOSES

Moses was a messianic symbol. The Angel connected to him must have been a messianic watcher to fulfill prophecy.

> *"Behold, I send an Angel before thee, to keep thee in the way, and to bring thee into the place which I have prepared. Beware of him, and obey his voice, provoke him not; for he will not pardon your transgressions: for my name is in him. But if thou shalt indeed obey his voice, and do all that I speak; then I will be an enemy unto*

thine enemies, and an adversary unto thine adversaries" (Exodus 23:20–22).

Watchers proclaim and connect to times and seasons. They clear the ground, create a healthy atmosphere, and cause the fulfillment of prophecy at the set time. Watchmen are the final ground troops who open the gates in the earth for the fulfillment of what the Watchers carry or even more, the word of God.

The Holy Ones, on the other hand, are connected to the twenty-four elders in heaven – Rev 4:4. They (heavenly elders) had human forms. They wore clothes and had crowns. All human traits. The Holy Ones were spirit messengers with human forms just like the twenty-four elders.

> *"Then there came again and touched me one like the appearance of a man, and he strengthened me," (Daniel 10:18).*

It is like the priesthood of Jesus named after the order of Melchizedek – Hebrews 6:20. The Holy Ones seem to carry the same pattern of the priesthood as the twenty-four elders but as messengers along with the Watchers of the Most High. They were not men but carried the face of men. That meant they were spirits.

In Daniel 8:13, the saint referred to in the king

James Version of the Bible is referred to as a Holy One in the Holman version and was referring to a spirit, not man, which agrees with Daniel 10:18 about spirits or angels in the human form being sent to carry messages in the earth. Abraham met with them. On their way to Sodom and Gomorrah, they branched to chat with him. Angels in human form. So there are angels who operate in human form to fulfill prophecy. They are not men, they are spirits.

3

OTHER WATCHERS
AND WATCHMEN

Tʜere are watchers and watchmen who restrain or hold back events. There are angels with measuring lines; that measure both judgment and prosperity. They either set boundaries or hold boundaries.

> *"The desert owl and the screech owl will possess it, and the great owl and the raven will dwell there. The Lord will stretch out a measuring line and a plumb line over her for destruction and chaos." (Isaiah 34:11 - HCSB)*

Job 26:10 says *"He hath compassed the waters with bounds until the day and night come to an end."* Watchmen are those whom the Lord uses to make creation and nature keep His appointed times and seasons.

"And after these things I saw four angels standing on the four corners of the earth, holding the four winds of the earth, that the wind should not blow on the earth, nor on the sea, nor on any tree" (Revelation 7:1).

"And he brought me thither, and, behold, there was a man, whose appearance was like the appearance of brass, with a line of flax in his hand, and a measuring reed; and he stood in the gate. And the man said unto me, Son of man, behold with thine eyes, and hear with thine ears, and set thine heart upon all that I shall shew thee; for to the intent that I might shew them unto thee, art thou brought hither: declare all that thou seest to the house of Israel.

And behold a wall on the outside of the house round about and in the man's hand a measuring reed of six cubits long by the cubit and an hand breadth: so he measured the breadth of the building, one reed; and the height, one reed." (Ezekiel 40:3-5)

"And the measuring line shall yet go forth over against it upon the hill Gareb and shall compass about to Goath." (Jeremiah 31:39)

"I lifted up mine eyes again, and looked, and behold a man with a measuring line in his hand." (Zechariah 2:1)

"For who scorns the day of small things? These seven eyes of the Lord, which scan throughout the whole earth, will rejoice when they see the plumb line in Zerubbabel's hand." (Zechariah 4:10 HCSB)

"He cried also in mine ears with a loud voice, saying, Cause them that have charge over the city to draw near, even every man with his destroying weapon in his hand. And, behold, six men came from the way of the higher gate, which lieth toward the north, and every man a slaughter weapon in his hand; and one man among them was clothed with linen, with a writer's inkhorn by his side: and they went in, and stood beside the brasen altar. And the glory of the God of Israel was gone up from the cherub, whereupon he was, to the threshold of the house. And he called to the man clothed with linen, which had the writer's inkhorn by his side; And the Lord said unto him, Go through the midst of the city, through the midst of Jerusalem, and set a mark upon the foreheads of the men that sigh and

that cry for all the abominations that be done in the midst thereof" (Ezekiel 9:1 - 4).

The Watchman's work, therefore, is to invite these WATCHERS to ESTABLISH and ENFORCE God's statues and bring down His seasons of visitations on the earth. For thus sayeth the Lord, to the Watchman,

> *"Look at the nations and observe— be utterly astounded! For something is taking place in your days that you will not believe when you hear about it." (Habakkuk 1:5 HCSB)*

> *"This is what the LORD says: I will answer you in a time of favor, and I will help you in the day of salvation. I will keep you, and I will appoint you to be a covenant for the people, to restore the land, to make them possess the desolate inheritances, saying to the prisoners: Come out, and to those who are in darkness: Show yourselves. They will feed along the pathways, and their pastures will be on all the barren heights. They will not hunger or thirst, the scorching heat or sun will not strike them; for their compassionate One will guide them, and lead them to springs of water. I will make all My mountains into a road, and My highways will be raised up." (Isaiah 49:8-11)*

"Look, it will be like a lion coming up from the thickets of the Jordan to the perennially watered grazing land. Indeed, I will chase Babylon away from her land in a flash. I will appoint whoever is chosen for her. For who is like Me? Who will summon Me? Who is the shepherd who can stand against Me?" (Jer 50:44)

"He has delivered us from such a terrible death, and He will deliver us; we have placed our hope in Him that He will deliver us again. And you can join in helping with a prayer for us, so that thanks may be given by many on our behalf for the gift that came to us through the prayers of many." (2 Cor 1:10-11 HCSB)

"Be not afraid of their faces: for I am with thee to deliver thee, saith the LORD. *Then the* LORD *put forth his hand and touched my mouth. And the* LORD *said unto me, Behold, I have put my words in thy mouth. See, I have this day set thee over the nations and over the kingdoms, to root out, and to pull down, and to destroy, and to throw down, to build, and to plant." (Jeremiah 1:8-10)* **AMEN!**

TESTIMONIES & PICTORIALS

ANTIGUA & BARBUDA

Apostle Kure with Hon. Baldwin Spencer, the
then Prime Minister of Antigua

Apostle Kure with Hon. Baldwin Spencer (first from left),
the then Prime Minister of Antigua at the Antigua
Recreation Grounds in a conference hosted by Ministers of
Flaming Fire – Pastors from different denominations –
February 2014.

WATCHMEN AS THE SHOFAR OF GOD

"All ye inhabitants of the world, and dwellers on the earth, see ye when he lifteth up an ensign on the mountains; and when he bloweth a trumpet, hear ye." (Isaiah 18:3)

God commands the earth to listen to His Watchmen whom He refers to as His ensign or messengers. It is a command to listen when they "blow the trumpet" accompanied by a word of prophecy.

"And it came to pass on the third day in the morning, that there were thunders and lightnings, and a thick cloud upon the mount, and the voice of the trumpet exceeding loud; so that

all the people that was in the camp trembled." (Exodus 19:16)

According to Exodus 19 verse 16, the shofar (trumpet) is God's own sound (voice) in the midst of the noise that preceded everything else and made way for the voice of God to be heard. It controls the lightnings and thunderings and their actions. The trumpet has its spirit language and speaks it in the hands of the righteous. Its voices are attached to answered prayers of saints.

"And the smoke of the incense, which came with the prayers of the saints, ascended up before God out of the angel's hand. And the angel took the censer, and filled it with fire of the altar, and cast it into the earth: and there were voices, and thunderings, and lightnings, and an earthquake."
(Revelation 8:4-5)

Voices, thunderings, (fire), and earthquakes are sequences of God's answered prayers.

Sounds conjure spirits. Spirits from the sea. Spirits from the winds. Spirits from the altars of the land. He collects them from everywhere to do what the sounds command. If it is to do God's will, it will do God's will: to do man's will, it will do man's will: to do Satan's will, it will do Satan's will. By sounds, people's destinies can be stolen or established. It must always come from an altar (including you) to effectively mobilize angels to work. Sometimes there is the need to organize teams to carry the sound around the city or a nation or continent depending on the demand of the Voice of God in you – the Holy Spirit.

The SHOFAR:

- Announces the crowning of a king or ushers a crowned king.
- Intercedes and interferes – Zephaniah 1:16, Ezekiel 33:3-5 and 1 Corinthians 14:8
- Proclaims lordship
- Opens spiritual highways
- Summons spiritual and physical forces in heavenly and earthly places to war or to worship or both - Amos 3:6, Zechariah 9:14, and Hosea 8:1
- Paves way for the army – the Hosts of Heaven to pass.
- Ushers in worship, high praises and showcases the awesomeness of God.
- Summons the spirit of the Lamb of sacrifice – the Messiah. That is why it is called the ram horn with roots from Abraham and Isaac's sacrifice and the provision of a ram from heaven. The Messiah became the Lamb of Sacrifice. It calls the Spirit of His sacrifice to bare.

- Promulgates the end of the present world order and ushers in the reign of God's righteousness and Kingdom on earth - Daniel 2:44, 7:26-27; Revelation 12:10; Isaiah 51:16; 1 Corinthians 15:52
- The heavens answer to the sound of the trumpet from the mouth of the righteous - Zechariah 8:1.
- Is the sound of the Spirit speaking to both the physical and spiritual o Hebrews 12:19, Revelations 4:1
- Is used to announce new moons, jubilees, and the voice or presence of God - Leviticus 15:9, Psalm 81:3.

A Watchman can blow the trumpet and none (spirits and men) will answer because of sin – his and the peoples'. So, the Watchman cannot afford to abuse his office even when others do.

> *"They have blown the trumpet, even to make all ready; but none goeth to the battle: for my wrath is upon all the multitude thereof" (Ezekiel 7:14).*

I have heard a few say that the ram's horn is for the Jews only.

First, God's watchman is God's watchman whether he is a Jew or a Gentile. And the

Watchman uses the Ram Horn as one of his instruments of office, for it represents him and what he is called to do.

Secondly, is the simple answer of Galatians chapter three verse fourteen.

> *"That the blessing of Abraham might come on the Gentiles through Jesus Christ; that we might receive the promise of the Spirit through faith"* *(Galatians 3:14).*

Through Abraham, in Christ Jesus, we qualify.

Lastly, is Ezekiel chapter thirty-three verse seven.

> *"So thou, O son of man, I have set thee a watchman unto the house of Israel; therefore thou shalt hear the word at my mouth, and warn them from me."*

If God sets me up as a watchman, I am bound to use the instruments of the watchman in order to be effective.

> *"And when the voice of the trumpet sounded long and waxed louder and louder, Moses spake, and God answered him by a voice."* *(Exodus 19:19)*

"When the voice of the trumpet (shofar) sounded long and waxed louder, Moses spoke and God answered him by voice." So does the Watchman.

 The spirit of the shofar releases other spirits to do God's will.

> *"And the sixth angel sounded, and I heard a voice from the four horns of the golden altar which is before God, Saying to the sixth angel which had the trumpet, Loose the four angels which are bound in the great river Euphrates" (Revelation 9:13-14).*

We must begin to address our nations as spirits as every name has a spirit attached to it. So, do the names of your nations. The Spirit of God in your voice (shofar) takes other spirits captive to do God's will – Rev. 9:13-14 including the spirit of the name of your nations to wipe away the names of Baalim.

> *"For I will take away the names of Baalim out of her mouth, and they shall no more be remembered by their name" (Hosea 2:17).*

Every name has a spirit behind it or a spiritual attraction (connotation) to it. We must begin to address our continents by name and their foundations, and command them (name and foundations) to let the people go! To let the people fulfill their destinies. Address them as spirits, not as mere names or continents. Call them and command them to let the people go! If you are from Africa, say, Africa! Let my people go! So that they may serve their destinies on earth.

> *"And I say unto thee, Let my son go, that he may serve me: and if thou refuse to let him go, behold, I will slay thy son, even thy firstborn." (Exodus 4:23)*

If you are from Europe, command Europe to let your people go. These are spirits, they will hear and let go. We must continue to demand that. Speak to their history, culture, and governments, and demand them to let the people go. Carry out prophetic actions as the prophets did over other nations in their days sealing these prayers. We must begin to pray a different kind of prayer in our time to meet the demands of the Lord for our time.

Europeans must command "Europe" to let them go to fulfill their divine purpose in history. So should the North American and Latin American Watchmen. So should all the other continents – Africa, Asia, North America, South America, Europe, Antarctica, and Australia/Oceania.

The Watchman must make the thrones of the Lord to sit over their nations and not give Him rest until He has turned their desolation around. When we begin this, movements will begin. The continents will begin to shift. Go round the continents, prophesy from one end to the other until something gives way and you see and experience the move of the Holy Spirit in your continent.

Even your name has a history, find its history, and make it conform to the purpose of your being alive.

Shofar Blown over South Africa Ushering it to a New Season from the Parliament – Cape Town.

Prophetic Reconciliations.   Breaking of yokes of disunity and dismantling the spiritual remnants of the apartheid era at the South African Parliament in Cape Town.

Opposition Party - Democratic Alliance leader, Mmusi Maimane, addressing the meeting.

Parliament Prayers – Cape Town, South Africa

INDONESIA

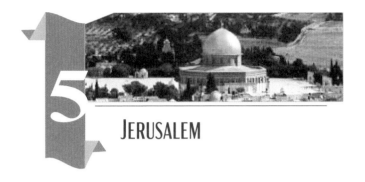

JERUSALEM

JIREH SHALL SEE TO THY PEACE!

Jerusalem is the "Mahanaim" of God. Mahanaim means the camp of God. The stones and mountains are about to be overturned, unveiled to reveal the ancient secrets. The books are about to be opened for armies to rise and gather from across the world. The seat of Melchizedek, King of Salem shall open up its secrets. Spirits have always dwelt side by side with men and rulers and it is about to beckon the world to do the Lord's bidding.

Seventy years after Jeremiah's prophecy, the heavens opened. From the time that

Daniel began to seek the face of the Lord, Angels started appearing on earth. The forces of good and evil also began to show themselves in response to Daniel's prayer to salvage a nation in order to ultimately fulfill the vision of a coming Messiah.

The Prince of Persia manifested to wage war with the Angel of God. Good kings and evil kings who were thrown in the world stage to battle against God's prophecy being fulfilled in man interfered with each other's flow. The die was cast. Heaven won and the temple was rebuilt after Nebuchadnezzar.

It took many bloodlines of kings, prophets, and God-fearing men including Esther and Darius to allow for and ensure that the temple was rebuilt. The temple, its stones, and tents represented Jehovah's dominion and His ownership and physical presence on earth. Abraham, Isaac, and Jacob built an altar wherever they went to open the doors of Heaven for God to visit and dwell with them. We are about to enter the dispensation when God will not only live in us through Christ Jesus but will be with us in the physical. The events that will usher that are beginning to unveil.

America's recognition of Jerusalem as the eternal capital of Israel following Israel's seventy years and the Knesset, Israel Parliament, gazetting Israel by a vote as a purely Jewish nation marks a rebirth is the KEY that unlocks the events that would unfold in Heaven and on earth. Note, the first nation and superpower that recognized Israel's independence in 1948 after Ben Gurion's declaration, by which the heavens and the earth went to war is again the first nation that recognizes her Biblical ancient capital as the "eternal" capital exactly seventy years after that declaration. That nation is America. This is a sign that a shift in the earth's history is about to take place. Nothing that happens on earth from now is isolated.

My spirit has been on the Lord's mountain and has beheld things that are too heavy to utter. Volumes of activity from the heavens and their effect and consequences that shall soon unfold all over the world, leave me in awe and fear daily. The Lord is asking me to be a participant and catalyst as a watchman, and not to stand on or by the lines while they happen.

> *"Who is there among you of all his people? his God be with him, and let him go up to Jerusalem, which is in Judah, and build the house of the LORD God of Israel, (he is the God,) which is in Jerusalem"* (Ezra 1:3).

The beginning of the building of the third temple and the events that will lead to it are about to be ushered in. The three events already have broken the seal. More unlockings are yet to come. As I visited the Temple Mount after the Rosh Hashanah of 5779 (2018) during the Feast of Tabernacles, there was a transcending Presence and feeling of urgent activity going on all around me at the place of the Golden Dome, that I did not feel like leaving the area.

Something was pulling me especially in places around the old well and where the old architect's office was and the second half of the dome. Something is not just normal there. There was a lot of spiritual activity going on all over Mt. Moriah, in abnormal dimensions and moments. Angels were descending and ascending, going on errands from that mountain.

Something was up! So, I took pictures peradventure I would notice or see anything abnormal in the pictures but I saw nothing. Yet I felt I was going through a spiritual crowd in that place and was being watched by eyes from beyond the veil of the physical.

Apostle Dr. Emmanuel Nuhu
Kure at Mount Moriah

We left from there to Ancient Shiloh and
while we were praying in a line formation,
facing the dugout ruins of where the
temple was believed to be situated, a man
suddenly appears and he claimed to be a
descendant of the priests, under Eli, who
served in that temple and also offered to
pray for us the "blessing" in the Jewish
language.

Was this a coincidence or was God trying
to say something? God told me that the
stones and the mountains of Jerusalem
are about to unveil their secrets which
they kept for ages for a time to come.

Ambassador-Designate, Drior Aydarey, a descendant of the Eli Priesthood Era, confirming our change of circles and seasons in Shiloh and praying a Hebraic blessing upon the people.

Joel 2:11-12 says,
> *"And the* LORD *shall utter his voice before his army: for his camp is very great: for he is strong that executeth his word: for the day of the* LORD *is great and very terrible; and who can abide it?"*

I sensed the convergence of Angels in Jerusalem and its environs. I sensed the call of the shofar has begun for forces of Heaven and the earth to emerge.

Something beyond human comprehension is about to happen in Jerusalem, even history will never be able to explain how it happened. Wars that don't make sense are about to be fought. Victories that will not make sense are about to be won. I keep hearing Isaiah 66 verses 8 and 9.

> *"Who hath heard such a thing? who hath seen such things? Shall the earth be made to bring forth in one day? or shall a nation be born at once? for as soon as Zion travailed, she brought forth her children. Shall I bring to the birth, and not cause to bring forth? saith the* LORD: *shall I cause to bring forth, and shut the womb? saith thy God"* (Isaiah 66:8-9).

This scripture is spoken over Jerusalem and the nations of the earth. God is about to birth a new thing! A major move of the Spirit as never seen before in world history is about to unveil that will turn the nations and world around. *"Behold, I will do a new thing; now it shall spring forth; shall ye not know it?"* (Isaiah 43:19a).

Jerusalem is founded on the bloodline of King Melchizedek, from whom Moses, David, Nebuchadnezzar, Darius, Yeshua (Jesus), and Hamashiach came from. The

Jebusites were the first to be mentioned in David's time but Melchizedek, King of Salem, had no beginning or end; he existed in a land where Angels once dwelt.

The attraction that led to all the crusades that were fought on that land was more than religious. It was the meeting point of spirits – a "Mahanaim" of the forces of Heaven led by the King of Heaven.

There is something different about Jerusalem city always that makes it peculiar from other cities of the world. There is a coolness; an aloofness and magnet around it that you cannot ignore or find anywhere else in the world.

The world needs to pay more attention to Jerusalem, to what it stands for, its message as the centerpiece of peace, AND HER GOD, if the world must find a balance.

Apostle Kure and his wife,
Pastor Martha Kure

Apostle Kure with the Nigeria Ambassador to
Israel, Amb. Enoch Duchi with his wife.

Apostle Dr. Kure baptizing pilgrims in
River Jordan, Israel

WATCHMEN OF GOD

"I appointed watchmen over you and said: Listen for the sound of the ram's horn. But they protested: We won't listen!" (Jeremiah 6:17).

The Watchman is the Ram's Horn (Trumpet) that God uses in every city. His duty is to make sounds while others listen and obey. Listen to the voice of the sound he is making if it is of God, obey. Whatever the Ram's Horn (Trumpet) represents in Heaven is what the Watchman represents on earth.

The Watchman is the revelation of Matthew 13:35 in the end times. Listen! Watch out for the sounds of God in the midst of the intrigues of the last days.

The sounds will show you the way, set you free, and bring you to your God!

The Watchman stays with God and is always in His presence. *"I was in the Spirit on the Lord's day and heard behind me a great voice, as of a trumpet"* (Revelation 1:10). The watchman hears, picks, or senses what **"Hashem"** is up to and acts appropriately. If he is in God's Throne when things are happening he could intercede to know what to do with what he sees or hears. The Holy Spirit or a divine messenger always responds to a Watchman's request. Revelation 4:2 says, *"And immediately I was in the spirit: and, behold, a throne was set in heaven, and one sat on the throne."*

Make a habit to stay in God's Presence and get to know God deeper. God carries you along to witness all He is doing or about to do.

> *"So he carried me away in the spirit into the wilderness: and I saw a woman sit upon a scarlet coloured beast, full of names of blasphemy, having seven heads and ten horns"* (Revelation 17:3).

Sometimes, the watchman is commanded by the Holy Spirit to run errands. At other times, he settles in God's presence to enjoy fellowship and immense revelations that will edify and clothe him with the wisdom of the One he loves so much.

He is drawn by pure love and worship for the Master.

One central trait of a true Watchman is that he enjoys staying in the presence of God for any given reason or at the slightest excuse. This helps him to notice things easily that others do not see; it develops his spiritual and physical senses to discern, see and hear things others do not. The practice of the things he hears, sees, or senses attracts the Spirit that speaks through his gifts. This makes him an oracle of God. The Holy Spirit of God occupies him, instructs, or takes charge of him from within to rule without.

All Watchmen work for and prepare the way for the Messiah, and particularly for His Kingdom programs. Watchmen clear the way and open spiritual and physical doors for people to prosper. Isaiah 61:6-10 says:

> *"But ye shall be named the Priests of the Lord: men shall call you the Ministers of our God: ye shall eat the riches of the Gentiles, and in their glory shall ye boast yourselves. For your shame, ye shall have double, and for confusion, they shall rejoice in their portion: therefore in their land,*

they shall possess the double: everlasting joy shall be unto them. For I the Lord love judgment, I hate robbery for burnt offering; and I will direct their work in truth, and I will make an everlasting covenant with them. And their seed shall be known among the Gentiles, and their offspring among the people: all that see them shall acknowledge them, that they are the seed which the Lord hath blessed. I will greatly rejoice in the Lord, my soul shall be joyful in my God; for he hath clothed me with the garments of salvation, he hath covered me with the robe of righteousness, as a bridegroom decketh himself with ornaments, and as a bride adorneth herself with her jewels."

WATCHMEN AS SERVANTS OF CHRIST

Watchmen serve Jesus, His Church, and the nations they are sent to. You must first of all know and remember that all creation including people and nations were made to serve a divine purpose. God deliberately situated all NATIONS after the fall of Adam, including the Gentile nations. The Watchman serves to fulfill His purpose as God's measuring line on earth.

"By these were the isles of the Gentiles divided in their lands; every one after his tongue, after their families, in their nations" (Genesis 10:5).

"And hath made of one blood all nations of men for to dwell on all the face of the earth, and hath determined the times before appointed, and the bounds of their habitation" (Acts 17:26).

"For who hath despised the day of small things? For they shall rejoice, and shall see the plummet in the hand of Zerubbabel with those seven; they are the eyes of the Lord, which run to and fro through the whole earth" (Zechariah 4:10).

Zerubbabel had a combination of God's "plummet" that makes the Angels meant to fulfill prophecy in heaven and on earth to serve. The Seven Spirits of Jesus in Revelations 5:6, sent to all the earth to serve Him. The Watchman, like Zerubbabel, is supposed to measure to the earth what God has measured to her, create or prophesy boundaries against excesses that God has not ordained, so that the enemy does not cross the line before his time.

The above factor is in order to avoid things that should be happening in the days of the Anti-Christ, happening now. He establishes signposts to give nations direction and guide them to the fullness and fulfillment of all that God has purposed in their destinies. The ultimate purpose of the Watchman is to bring people and nations to the fullness of what was programmed for them in this world and in the world to come.

WATCHMEN IN THE FIVEFOLD MINISTRY

Watchmen are drawn from the five-fold ministries of Apostles, Prophets, Pastors, E v a n g e l i s t s a n d Teachers by the Holy Spirit. When God sends them watchmen, He can make them operate in any of the five-fold ministries just to fulfill His mission.

Watchmen are not limited by any office. If the mission requires the Watchman to take the attributes of a prophet to fulfill it, he becomes a prophet for that moment and purpose. If it requires him to be an evangelist, apostle, teacher, or pastor, he wears the attributes of those offices to fulfill his mission. Isaiah at a point was required to go naked. He went naked for three years. Ezekiel slept sideways for a particular period and turned to the other side for another particular period. Hosea was asked to marry a whore – prostitute. He did with repercussions to his emotional life just to pass the Lord's message. That is the lot of the Watchman.

The Watchman and possibly his children are for signs and wonders in the hands of our great God.

> "*The voice of the Lord calls out to the city (and it is wise to fear Your name): "Pay attention to the rod and the One who ordained it"* (Micah 6:9, HSBC).

Observe closely the pattern and manner God's Rod operates in the city and you will notice something and receive an understanding. Seek His face about it, and then you can choose the line of action He prescribes. His Spirit will step into the situation to bring it to the requested end.

If you observe closely, you will "see" the rod and know who has appointed it, and what to do about it. Three things mentioned in the King James Version that Watchmen must note are SEE NAME, HEAR ROD, DECERN WHO SENT IT OR WHO IS BEHIND IT before you act or decide a line of action.

Questions you must first ask yourself is what would the Lord want me to do? Does He want me to hold my peace, put it to heart, or act? Is it just for my information, as a friend converses with his friend and father to son? Or for me to do something about it? These are the questions you must answer whenever you SEE and HEAR anything when interceding for the nation.

Your mission is to do right for your nation and secure the future of her people on all grounds. You are to guarantee peace and security by whatever shakings and overhauls the Lord brings, not on religious grounds. You must downplay religion in nation-building without undermining it.
Find a balance. Emphasis should be on righteousness.

LEVIATHAN

The Watchman is always in confrontation with those who arouse Leviathan. Especially those who practice all kinds of divination, Christians or not.

> *"Let those who curse certain days cast a spell on it, those who are skilled in rousing Leviathan." (Job 3:8 HCSB)*

There are demons whose only work is to trouble people in the day, and demons whose only work is to trouble people in the night.

There are those whose divination attempt to control the lives and destinies of men and nations using daily spells and enchantments.

There are demons sent from hell, off-springs of Leviathan to make the day a tortuous experience.

You wake up and things start spinning out of control. Attacks from everywhere. The day-demon is at work. They torment everything they meet and taunt those with the mark of God to see whether they will give up their guard and expose their weakness for an attack. They make sure that everything that can go wrong, goes wrong.

> *"Surely he shall deliver thee from the snare of the fowler, and from the noisome pestilence. He shall cover thee with his feathers, and under his wings shalt thou trust: his truth shall be thy shield and buckler. Thou shalt not be afraid for the terror by night; nor for the arrow that flieth by day; Nor for the pestilence that walketh in darkness; nor for the destruction that wasteth at noonday." (Psalm 91:3-6)*

They are the ones David was referring to in Psalms 91:3-6. They attack his every move and become pests in his life. Paul called them buffeting spirits. This is why the Bible insists that "the sun shall not smite thee by day, nor the moon by night" – Psalm 121:6. David was exposing us to the activities of demons called Deber and Qeteb in Psalm 91 scripture who take advantage of the sun and moon to attack and make life miserable for men.

The root word for "pestilence" in verse six is Qeteb and for "destruction" is Deber. They descend on men immediately day breaks to make their lives miserable. Satan feeds from our misery. You must not allow him to feed on you. Men, according to Job 3:8, release them to change the course of things and tilt results in favor of Satan.

The day demon orchestrates mental stress and physical agitations by day. They tend to drive people mad. Get them irritated and agitated for no just cause. You just find yourself getting angry or irritated without a genuine reason. It is "Qeteb" at work. You wake up one day and you find that everything that can go wrong goes wrong. It brings unexplainable violence to men and makes people lose mental control to carry out actions they regret later.

Rebuke them in the first instance. Don't wait. When you sense anger in the day time without a cause, plead the blood of Jesus to control yourself. It is a spirit provoking you to violence. People have been victims of this violence without a cause. They make peaceful protests violent with sometimes devastating effects. They make strange accidents happen, disrupt people's daily programs.

They create pits and troubles you did not think of when you woke up. Quarrels and stabbings. Sudden temperaments. Sudden chest pains in the day time. That is Qeteb at work. Every form of losing control by day is from the spirit of Qeteb. He uses an arrow, shoots at people, and waits for their lives to be violently disrupted.

You will notice that people with mental disorders are mostly agitated and affected during the day and more peaceful at night. That is the spirit of Qeteb. They work with the forces of the day to wreak havoc. They are part of the wind demons. They scourge the brain to lose control. They cause sunstroke. And bring misfortune by day. Rebuke, bind and cast out or break the spell, and calm will come. Or pray for peace over water and give it to the agitated and peace will come. Whatever you do, break their spell by day.

Strongs Exhaustive Concordance says the word pestilence in this particular verse is actually the name of a demon called Qeteb in its root rendition while the word destruction is Deber in its root rendition. Both are spirits of day and night.

Prophets and Apostles should beware of Qeteb. He distracts them with a violent emotion and the power of their message is destroyed, or distracts them with anger to distract them. Qeteb is normally known as the spirit of commotion. He smites people with madness.

Deber, the night demon, promotes fear and sleeplessness because of anxiety. The one-eyed Deber with the second eye said to be in the middle of his heart was often referred to in ancient times as "the poisonous Deber." He strikes people with fear and deep anxieties at night. Some whose fevers only come at night with the fear of death, without any physical cause to show for it is an affliction from the night demon Deber.

They steal and distort dreams to make sure that the interpretation is misrepresented. They distort destiny. See T. H. Gaster, Demons, Demonology, 1969: page 770 and Dictionary of Deities and Demons in the Bible, 1999 Second Extensive Revised Edition Page 572. Strongs Exhaustive Concordance – H6986 and H1696.

When your day keeps on being disrupted, you will have to deal with these demons to get back your peace. Deber walks (Psalm 91:6) in darkness and brings plagues and afflictions to people. Most misfortunes at night are caused by Deber. The Holman version calls them "the plagues that stalk in darkness or the pestilence that ravages at noonday."

There are people that these demons possess to bring trouble to you without cause. They make them transfer aggression for reasons even they cannot fully explain or understand. You deal with these people daily.

No wonder God tied His covenant of day and night to the personal covenant He made with David in Jeremiah 33:20-26 to protect him from these evil disruptions of the day and night. See my other book – Practical Prophetic Prayer and Warfare or download it from the Kindle Store.

Openly Burning Witchcraft Books and Paraphernalia in Eliot, Maine, USA – 2010

"Thus saith the LORD; If ye can break my covenant of the day and my covenant of the night, and that there should not be day and night in their season;

Then may also my covenant be broken with David my servant, that he should not have a son to reign upon his throne; and with the Levites the priests, my ministers. As the host of heaven cannot be numbered, neither the sand of the sea measured: so will I multiply the seed of David my servant, and the Levites that minister unto me. Moreover, the word of the LORD came to Jeremiah, saying, Considerest thou not what this people have spoken, saying, The two families which the LORD hath chosen, he hath even cast them off? thus they have despised my people, that they should be no more a nation before them. Thus saith the LORD; If my covenant be not with day and night, and if I have not appointed the ordinances of heaven and earth; Then will I cast away the seed of Jacob, and David my servant, so that I will not take any of his seed to be rulers over the seed of Abraham, Isaac, and Jacob: for I will cause their captivity to return, and have mercy on them."

(Jeremiah 33:20-26)

You must also make God link His covenant with you day and night to protect you from these disruptive spirits so that you can fulfill your destiny without "unforeseen circumstances."

This was also why Job was asked to command the morning to disrupt evil men and spirits daily if he wanted to rule the day. See my book – Apostolic Invasion.

> *"Hast thou commanded the morning since thy days, and caused the dayspring to know his place; that it might take hold of the ends of the earth, that the wicked might be shaken out of it?" (Job 38:12-13)*

Lastly, you need to unleash the hunters of heaven to go after them and destroy their works.

> *"Behold, I will send for many fishers, saith the LORD, and they shall fish them; and after will I send for many hunters, and they shall hunt them from every mountain, and from every hill, and out of the holes of the rocks." (Jeremiah 16:16)*

Command these hunters and fishers of heaven to go after them. Start your day by asking God's hunters to clear them out of your day and for the Holy Spirit to guide your path and redeem you. It will make your business go faster and smoother without interference. These revelations come handy in land deliverance. Leviathan drops demons in territories to serve specific duties. We will deal with this in another book.

We were on a prophetic prayer drive convoy around the city of Cincinnati when I stumbled on an ancient grave at a major popular cemetery bearing the name "Deber." It was a shocking discovery for me as the date on the tombstone was since early last century. The owner must have come from a physical genealogy of warlocks who have their roots from the famed fallen giants. I still cannot get over that reality of the evidence of these families of giants having their graves among us, and that their physical ancestors might be next-door neighbors.

It meant that right there in Cincinnati, USA, there are families with giant fallen demon's DNA existing. I shuddered. The reality came home to me. That must have been God's reason for sending me to Cincinnati. I took the picture of that tombstone but cannot find it now. We drove around inside that big cemetery and stopped once or twice to pray and praise at strategic places particularly at the point where the obelisk stood and a few other demonic high places in the cemetery.

It is from some of those places that demon worshipers exact control over nations and cities and people and conjure spirits to rule, connecting with ancestral and historical demons. We had to break the veil cast over the city from there and from the sea.

Burning Satanic Mediums in Cincinnati, USA – 2009

Breaking Yokes and Opening Doors of Glory Over Florida at a Tallahassee Borderline.

The Watchman must practically learn from his stay in the presence of God how to practically biblically deal with these disruptive powers. The Watchman must NOT leave the confines of the

Holy Spirit and the Holy Bible when dealing with these issues lest a strange spirit hijacks the process to serve Satan's purpose. The temptation there is to seek further clarifications from strange demonic books or the seven books of Moses or strange books on angels not mentioned in the Bible.

All authority not gotten from the place of prayer and the WORD (Bible) is a strange authority. It is easy to cross the line, so the watchman must beware! The watchers, which include Gabriel and Michael, are some of the angels put at the disposal of the Watchman. The Holy Spirit or the Father assigns them to work with the Watchman. They will NOT do anything that does not align with the Father and His Word. Be warned!

To conclude this chapter, there are men and spirits whose business is to conjure these disruptive spirits daily into their activities – Job 3:8. The Watchman is the other side of God's Arm that stops these spirits in society. Let us rise to the task ahead of us.

NOTE: It is very important that the Watchman must take advantage of every assignment and pulpit opportunity to win souls and convert men to Christ. It is in bringing them to Christ that they are translated from the reach of these forces of darkness.

Any watchman without the burning passion to save souls from (self) destruction to the eternal path of righteousness is not a called watchman. He is always compassionate and passionate to do God's will both in his spiritual and secular life. The Watchman is the angelic arm of humanity that keeps the sanctity of God's Word in human life.

PROPHETIC ACTION

Watchmen sometimes (ONLY AT THE INSTANCE OF THE HOLY SPIRIT) symbolically break pots, jars, bottles, sticks, etc., after prophesying the WORD into them to break the ordinance and hold of enchanters over cities, nations, or people as a result of the sorcery of witches and those that practice divination. It is called Prophetic Action.

Just like Jesus spat on the soil and asked the blind man to wash. He would have chosen to lay hands on him or better still just speak the word! But He connected to dust (nature) from which he came to set him free. Sometimes watchmen are commanded to do stuff like that where serious sorcery is involved. Read my other books for further explanations. Jeremiah used symbols a lot in his time. So did Ezekiel, Agabus, God Himself in Peter's dream, to break spells or pass God's words or seal God's judgment.

"Thus saith the LORD, Go and get a potter's earthen bottle, and take of the ancients of the people, and of the ancients of the priests; and go forth unto the valley of the son of Hinnom, which is by the entry of the east gate, and proclaim there the words that I shall tell thee, and say, Hear ye the word of the LORD, O kings of Judah, and inhabitants of Jerusalem; Thus saith the LORD of hosts, the God of Israel; Behold, I will bring evil upon this place, the which whosoever heareth, his ears shall tingle. because they have forsaken me, and have estranged this place, and have burned incense in it unto other gods, whom neither they nor their fathers have known, nor the kings of Judah, and have filled this place with the blood of innocents; they have built also the high places of Baal, to burn their sons with fire for burnt offerings unto Baal, which I commanded not, nor spake it, neither came it into my mind: Therefore, behold, the days come, saith the LORD, that this place shall no more be called Tophet, nor The valley of the son of Hinnom, but The valley of slaughter. And I will make void the counsel of Judah and

Jerusalem in this place; and I will cause them to fall by the sword before their enemies, and by the hands of them that seek their lives: and their carcasses will I give to be meat for the fowls of the heaven, and for the beasts of the earth. And I will make this city desolate, and a hissing; every one that passeth thereby shall be astonished and hiss because of all the plagues thereof. And I will cause them to eat the flesh of their sons and the flesh of their daughters, and they shall eat every one the flesh of his friend in the siege and straitness, wherewith their enemies, and they that seek their lives, shall straiten them. Then shalt thou break the bottle in the sight of the men that go with thee," (Jeremiah 19:1-10)

Read between all the verses from one to ten to see the message that his prophetic action activated and their spiritual ramifications. God had to use unclean animals to break Peter's Hebraic spell that was founded on the laws of Moses.

Prophetic Open Heavens Prayer Action, Eliot,
Tallahassee Border Witchcraft Maine – 2010

Apostle Bunmi Akomolede – Throneroom –
Houston, USA

7

TRAP:
THE VALLEY OF VISION

" *bewilderment in the Valley of Vision—* *For the Lord GOD of Hosts had a day of tumult, trampling, and people shouting and crying to the mountains*" (Isaiah 22:5, HCSB)

There is a Valley of Vision where the Watchman sometimes lives. Be careful not to be trapped in it. Be careful to allow the WORD to navigate your way through it. Many have lost their way while some have gotten so enmeshed in visions and dreams such that the Holy Scriptures become secondary to visions.

They misinterpret visions, thereby bring the name of the Lord to disrepute thereby making people to doubt prophecy and the Word of God. These are those who are trapped in the valley of visions.

Make no mistake, there is a valley of vision. Don't get sucked into it. When one gets sucked into it, he lives in hallucination, and his imagination; and has mistaken it for a real vision.

It becomes a state of mind. This is dangerous. Many are drawn into this state when they feel insecure about reality. They find succor or attempt to create hope through visions, dreams, and revelations.

The demonic world often takes advantage of this to turn them into oracles of the Fallen One – Lucifer – who pretends or comes in as an angel of light.

The visions that come from these people sometimes sound real and other times offish but are always contrary to scriptures or even opposed to it, and yet look godly.

Many of them call themselves seers. There are no seers in the Church of the New Testament. There are only prophets (1 Corinthians 12:28, Ephesians 4:10-11) who through visions and dreams plus the word of God (Holy Scriptures) prophesy aided by the revelation gifts like the Word of Wisdom, Word of Knowledge, Gift of Prophecy, Gift of Tongues, and Interpretation of Tongues.

Seers are not mentioned in the new covenant of Jesus as they can easily fall prey to fallen demons or are caught in the valley of visions.

Genuine visions and revelations are borne out of intense prayer, communion with God, and an in-depth study of the Word. A person given to prayer and the Word will always have revelations and instructions from God.

Revelation is the Third Voice outside your thoughts (mind) and desires (flesh). The Third Voice is the still small voice that breaks through your thoughts and desires to caution, direct, and instruct you. And when you heed to it, you do not go wrong. The Lord uses your abundance of fellowship with Him to guide you.

The Valley of Vision is a REALM where people who dream or see visions can get trapped. Unless the Word of God pulls them out, they may never come out of it, but build a world of their own in that REALM. Satan traps the souls and minds of his victims when they begin to believe in visions and dreams more than the Word of God.

Destinies of people are caught up and cut off in this valley. Those who live by dreams in their sleep or visions are victims of this. Their blessings are hindered by the walls this valley has created.

I pray for those whose destinies have been shut in the valley of dreams to be set free now in Jesus' name! There shall be no more interferences in your dream in Jesus' name! No more keeping the balance word out of your interpretations in Jesus' name!

It is the duty of Watchmen and faithful believers to find the victims and disconnect them from that demonic trap and stronghold.

> *"And God said, Let there be a firmament in the midst of the waters, and let it divide the waters from the waters. And God made the firmament, and divided the waters which were under the firmament from the waters which were above the firmament: and it was so. And God called the firmament Heaven. And the evening and the morning were the second day"* (Genesis 1:6-8).

Release God's firmaments to separate the victims' dreams and cut off the familiar spirit in Jesus' name. Their minds should be sanctified, cleansed, and renewed by the Word of God and by the Blood of Jesus.

Let the Blood of Jesus be sprinkled on them in the spirit realm. Break holy bread with them and reconnect their spirits and souls to that of Christ and they are set free. This is in line with 1st Peter 1:2 and Hebrews 12:24.

> *"Elect according to the foreknowledge of God the Father, through*

sanctification of the Spirit, unto obedience and sprinkling of the blood of Jesus Christ: Grace unto you, and peace, be multiplied" (1 Peter 1:2).

"And to Jesus the mediator of the new covenant, and to the blood of sprinkling, that speaketh better things than that of Abel" (Hebrews 12:24).

The Blood divides realms of reality. It carries the power of God that gives us GRACE in our physical world.

The Blood of Jesus and the Word form the firmament that separates worlds and realities. You can use this understanding to pray for those with a mental disorder, to break the power of the two worlds and two realities they live in. May the Lord give you the WISDOM to handle the victims of the valley of visions and set them free from demonic bondage.

Note Please – true dreams that are genuinely from God will need to be activated by obedience or prophetic action on the part of the dreamer.

Gideon was reacting to a dream when he set three hundred men with trumpets and pitchers.

He translated or brought or activated it by the prophetic action of cutting loose these three hundred on Saul. The soldiers of Saul turned against each other. What a reaction to prophetic action. Because heaven comes alive at the beginning of every watch, prophetic actions are most effective at the beginning of a watch, not just anytime.

Apostle Dr. Kure Praying at the Gate of Time – Tema, Ghana

8

THE WATCHMAN AND DEMONS

From ancient times there has been a battle between man and principalities over the control of the earth. Each community must at some point confront these principalities who seek to distort her destiny and bring great suffering to the community. The community that lacks called men to stand against these evil spirits in human form becomes a den or dwelling place of evil until the day it is delivered. God said, "I looked for a man who will stand in the gap." Watchmen are the only ones who can stand between evil overrunning the societies from time immemorial.

The Fallen Demons recorded in Revelations Chapter 12 and Genesis Chapter 6 were thrown out of Heaven and they decided to come after the sons of men to revenge; they war against God by destroying and corrupting everything He created. Some of them even settled down with men in Noah's time, thereby polluting the world with great wickedness.

These demons formed themselves into principalities of the communities where they settled or migrated in time. And because they are part of the spiritual wickedness in "heavenly places" they attempt to influence things after the lust of their father (the devil) in the hope that God who is too righteous to behold iniquity will let go when He can no longer stop the flow of sin and their corruption of all things. They succeeded in making the people lust after the flesh and corrupt things, forgetting the Scripture that:

> "*He setteth an end to darkness, and searcheth out all perfection: the stones of darkness, and the shadow of death*" (Job 28:3).

THE SPIRIT OF PROPHECY

Jesus is the SPIRIT of Time and Prophecy.
Every one of God's programs is connected to TIME.

> *"And I fell at his feet to worship him.
> And he said unto me, See thou do it
> not: I am thy fellow servant, and of
> thy brethren that have the testimony
> of Jesus: worship God: for the
> testimony of Jesus is the spirit of
> prophecy" (Revelation 19:10).*

Prophecy means time. Time could be in the past, present, or future; time also controls the unknown. When the TIME comes, Jesus will consume them with the Spirit of His mouth.

> *"And then shall that Wicked be revealed,
> whom the Lord shall consume with the spirit*

> *of his mouth, and shall destroy with the*
> *brightness of his coming"* (2 Thessalonians
> 2:8).

The greatest weapon of the Watchman is the Spirit of the mouth of Christ which has the power to contain, control, create, destroy, and build. It can create a new heaven and a new earth.

> *"And I have put my words in thy*
> *mouth, and I have covered thee in the*
> *shadow of mine hand, that I may*
> *plant the heavens, and lay the*
> *foundations of the earth, and say*
> *unto Zion, Thou art my people"* (Isaiah
> 51:16).

Every Watchman has a spirit in his mouth. The language by which he defeats Satan and demons is the Scriptures his heart has conceived and mouth can utter. The language God has cultivated from his many prayers and wrestling with Him that comes out naturally laced with scriptures and revelation that he speaks each time he is in a deep battle with Satan will overcome every situation.

Words that flow naturally by revelation from your heart in the heat of battle are the spirit of your mouth. The Holy Ghost puts words in your mouth in the heat of your agony and travail. The Spirit of God rides on this to crush the principality that stands against you.

God will create and cultivate this in many Christians for the battle and conquest ahead. Learn to pray with Scriptures when you travail or groan in your spirit. With time, Scriptures become spirit and life and will take hold of fallen principalities. Scriptures that you have stored in your heart carry power. And what comes from your heart if executed, controls your circumstances.

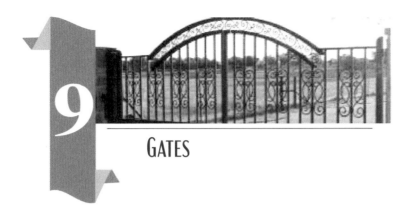

9

GATES

"And I also say to you that you are Peter, and on this rock, I will build My church, and the gates of Hades shall not prevail against it" (Matthew 16:18)

"Now the two angels came to Sodom in the evening, and Lot was sitting in the gate of Sodom. When Lot saw them, he rose to meet them, and he bowed himself with his face toward the ground" (Genesis 19:1).

"And delivered righteous Lot, who was oppressed by the filthy conduct of the wicked (for that righteous man, dwelling among them, tormented his righteous soul from day to day by seeing and hearing their lawless

deeds) — then the Lord knows how to deliver the godly out of temptations and to reserve the unjust under punishment for the day of judgment" (2 Peter 2:7-9).

"Now David was sitting between the two gates. And the watchman went up to the roof over the gate, to the wall, lifted his eyes and looked, and there was a man, running alone" (2 Samuel 18:24).

"For behold, I am calling all the families of the kingdoms of the north," says the LORD; *"They shall come and each one set his throne at the entrance of the gates of Jerusalem, against all its walls all around, and against all the cities of Judah"* (Jeremiah 1:15).

"And I will winnow them with a winnowing fan in the gates of the land; I will bereave them of children; I will destroy My people, since they do not return from their ways" (Jeremiah 15:7a).

"Thus the LORD said to me: "Go and stand in the gate of the children of the people, by which the kings of Judah

come in and by which they go out, and in all the gates of Jerusalem" (Jeremiah 17:19).

"This city shall not be your caldron, nor shall you be the meat in its midst. I will judge you at the border of Israel" (Ezekiel 11:11).

David used gates to establish both spiritual and physical command. He sat by the gate to monitor events day and night. Note that the control button is always at the gates of nations at all times and in all situations. Find the gates within and without if you want to rule in your nation. The Gates control human direction but the Lord controls our existence. Everything indeed has its gate.

See Proverbs 8:34, Songs of Solomon 7:13; Isaiah 26:2, 45:1-2, 60:11 & 18, 62:10; Nahum 2:6.

Creation is waiting for Watchmen who will command, insist, and dominate.

"For the earnest expectation of the creature waiteth for the manifestation of the sons of God." (Romans 8:19)

Communities also have human gates. For Paul to conquer Paphos he had to conquer sorcery (Elymas) in order to convert the soul of Sergius Paulus (the ruler) and have free entry into the city.

Both Elymas and Sergius were human doorways by which Paphos was ruled. This means that by controlling the ruler Sergius, Elymas controlled Paphos. Paul needed to take full charge spiritually and physically for the gospel to break through into Paphos.

You need to find human doorways into your territory; people who rule your communities, and families spiritually, and those who exercise physical governance, and dominate them before you can control the direction of that community or nation. Watchmen must seek the men in their cities who stand in the way of their city's prosperity.

> *"The evil bow before the good; and the wicked at the gates of the righteous."* (Proverbs 14:19)

> *"Lift ye up a banner upon the high mountain, exalt the voice unto them, shake the hand, that they may go into the gates of the nobles."* (Isaiah 13:2)

Gates are used to lock and unlock. So, every Watchman must go to the gates or the borders or its outskirts and release the Angels of the watches according to their courses (Judges 5:20-21) to do what they were assigned to do in their callings from the place of their dwellings.

By the Word of God, you will build and plant on earth and also rule over every creature on earth. *"And I have put my words in thy mouth, and I have covered thee in the shadow of mine hand, that I may plant the heavens, and lay the foundations of the earth, and say unto Zion, Thou art my people"* (Isaiah 51:16).

Judges 5:8 says,

> *"They chose new gods; then was war in the gates: was there a shield or spear seen among forty thousand in Israel?"*

Sons of God, angels, and men, fight this war and decide its outcome and dominion. Who are the sons of God? You may ask. The Bible says that Jesus is the first begotten of the Sons of God.

> "Who is the image of the invisible God, the firstborn of every creature:"
> (Colossians 1:13)

In Mark 1:1 He is called the Son of God and Mark 5:7 even demons call Him "Son of the Most High God." All Angels are also the sons of God.

> *"Now there was a day when the sons of God came to present themselves before the Lord, and Satan came also among them"* (Job 1:6).

Every believer in Christ is the son of God.

> *"Behold, what manner of love the Father hath bestowed upon us, that we should be called the sons of God: therefore the world knoweth us not, because it knew him not"* (1 John 3:1).

> *"But as many as received him, to them gave he power to become the sons of God, even to them that believe on his name"* (John 1:2).

> *"For as many as are led by the Spirit of God, they are the sons of God... For the earnest expectation of the creature waiteth for the manifestation of the sons of God."* (Romans 8:14, 19).

Creation waits for the sons of God to decide their fate. Romans 8:19 says that creation is waiting for "Sons of God." Sons of God should arise and join forces for the salvation of the world. Creation is waiting for the chosen men, who will collapse into one of the powers of the heavens and the earth through Christ Jesus to save the world.

Ephesians 1:10 says,

> *"That in the dispensation of the fulness of times he might gather together in one all things in Christ,*

*both which are in heaven, and which
are on earth; even in him."*

Even so, come quickly Lord Jesus! Come quickly oh Spirit of the Most High and let Your fire fall!

It is time to bring out your shields (God) and riding His chariots, sitting on the throne of the promises of the house of David and the Messiah, and advancing the forces of heaven into the nations to execute the judgments of God on the nations. To plant and to pull down, to build and to destroy. To set up new standards in the land by which the Lord shall rule.

THE LORD OUR SHIELD

*"Behold, O God our shield, and look
upon the face of thine anointed"*
(Psalm 84:9).

Get ready to go to the borders and gates to proclaim liberty to the captive and release them from the bondage of sin. Establish the hand of God and the fulfillment of the prophecies upon your lands.

Let the Angels of the seven churches and the Angels of the twelve tribes of Israel pull the forces of creation in all their fullness to our aid as a new world prepared for the Lord.

> *"Then shall there enter into the gates of this city kings and princes sitting upon the throne of David, riding in chariots and on horses, they, and their princes, the men of Judah, and the inhabitants of Jerusalem: and this city shall remain forever"* (Jeremiah 17:25).

> *"And had a wall great and high, and had twelve gates, and at the gates twelve angels, and names written thereon, which are the names of the twelve tribes of the children of Israel"* (Revelation 21:12).

Beware of the GATES OF TIME and the countries where they cross through to affect the seasons of nations. When the anti-Christ spirit begins to open new landmarks and gates to control human life, times, and seasons, then know that the day of the Lord is near. Beware of the anti-Christ opening new gates of time to replace or control the existing ones.

The Spirit of the Lord warns about the new landmarks that will tend to change ancient landmarks in order to overthrow God's hold on the earth. Great changes are happening in the gates of time that will seek to change times and seasons even beyond the religious and moral traditions.

The Watchman therefore must be ready to stand before the Lord and invoke the mystery of the "sundial" to control or change things.

> *"Behold, I will bring again the shadow of the degrees, which is gone down in the sundial of Ahaz, ten degrees backward. So the sun returned ten degrees, by which degrees it was gone down"* (Isaiah 38:8).

We need to have the power of God, like Isaiah, to speak into the sun and bring down the hand of God.

KENYA

Proclamations over the nations and Kenya hosted by Apostle John Kimani William and the Global Spheres International, Africa led by Bishop Geoffrey Njuguna and Bishop Othniel Nwabili at the Equator in Nanyuki, Kenya

Breaking pots and witchcraft over Kenya. Covenant of Salt for Kenya and the nations

The river "gate" in Haifa, Israel, which is the closest river gate to Armagedo is linked to River Euphrates where the great army that will fight the

Messiah at His coming might come out from. Places like this and surrounding rivers connected to the Euphrates should be watched and tackled prophetically until the appointed time.

> "And the sixth angel poured out his vial upon the great river Euphrates; and the water thereof was dried up, that the way of the kings of the east might be prepared. And I saw three unclean spirits like frogs come out of the mouth of the dragon, and out of the mouth of the beast, and out of the mouth of the false prophet. For they are the spirits of devils, working miracles, which go forth unto the kings of the earth and of the whole world, to gather them to the battle of that great day of God Almighty. Behold, I come as a thief. Blessed is he that watcheth, and keepeth his garments, lest he walk naked, and they see his shame. And he gathered them together into a place called in the Hebrew tongue Armageddon" (Revelation 16:12-16).

Apostle Kure with the Deputy
President of Kenya and his wife

Deputy President of Kenya, His
Excellency, William Ruto & family
Breaking Passover Bread.

Apostle John Kimani, Apostle
Kure & Archbishop Arthur Kitonga

WATCHES

The Angels carry out their tasks in the heavenly places as it concerns the earth during the Watches. They enter the earth from the gates of the Watches. Jesus rose in the morning watch hour. Peter received his Angelic visitors at the sixth hour – the beginning of a watch (Acts 10:9-20). Cornelius had an angelic visitation at the ninth hour (Acts 10:30). Most angelic visitations come at the time of prayer. You must create your prayer discussion hours and talk with God. The hours you wait on Him determines how much He talks to you. They open channels of discussion.

Every three hours according to timings of day and night, the spiritual portals or gates of Heaven open to the earth to connect; transmissions take place for one hour between Heaven and earth. I know this from the interaction Jesus had with His disciples at Gethsemane when He went to pray.

> *"And he cometh unto the disciples, and findeth them asleep, and saith unto Peter, What, could ye not watch with me one hour?"* (Matthew 26:40).

That first hour of every watch is a gate and portal where heavenly transmissions take place. The disciples missed it because their flesh was weak. The hours of prayer are referred to in the Bible as Watches. They go in symmetry of six, nine, twelve, three – six, nine, twelve, three, day and night. The Jews before the Roman invasion historically had only three watches – first (6-10 pm), middle (10-2 am) and morning (2-6 am) watch.

But at the advent of the Romans, the watches changed to four. Jesus operated during the Roman era. Interestingly, the Angels seemed to be operating at the same time meaning the Roman watch conformed to some astral spirit thing. The same way the three Magi saw from the star the birth of Jesus. The Romans believed in Astrology and its influence on the physical and spiritual.

> *"And it came to pass, that in the morning watch the LORD looked unto the host of the Egyptians through the pillar of fire and of the cloud, and troubled the host of the Egyptians"* (Exodus 14:24).

At the sixth watch, ninth watch, twelfth watch, or third watch, the portals open and the firmament divides the spiritual from the physical. The spirit deposits life and things that influence the directions and actions of men and earth.

"For these are not drunken, as ye suppose, seeing it is but the third hour of the day. But this is that which was spoken by the prophet Joel; And it shall come to pass in the last days, saith God, I will pour out of my Spirit upon all flesh: and your sons and your daughters shall prophesy, and your young men shall see visions, and your old men shall dream dreams:
And on my servants and on my handmaidens I will pour out in those days of my Spirit; and they shall prophesy" (Acts 2:15-18).

"On the morrow, as they went on their journey, and drew nigh unto the city, Peter went up upon the housetop to pray about the sixth hour: And he became very hungry, and would have eaten: but while they made ready, he fell into a trance, And saw heaven opened, and a certain vessel descending unto him, as it had been a great sheet knit at the four corners, and

let down to the earth" (Acts 10:9‑11). "And Cornelius said, Four days ago I was fasting until this hour; and at the ninth hour I prayed in my house, and, behold, a man stood before me in bright clothing" (Acts 10:30).

"Now Peter and John went up together into the temple at the hour of prayer, being the ninth hour" (Acts 3:1).

"And it was about the sixth hour, and there was a darkness over all the earth until the ninth hour. And the sun was darkened, and the veil of the temple was rent in the midst. And when Jesus had cried with a loud voice, he said, Father, into thy hands I commend my spirit: and having said thus, he gave up the ghost" (Luke 23:44-46).

"Now from the sixth hour, there was darkness over all the land unto the ninth hour. And about the ninth hour, Jesus cried with a loud voice, saying, Eli, Eli, lama sabachthani? That is to say, My God, my God, why hast thou forsaken me? Some of them that stood there, when they heard that, said, This man calleth for Elias. And straightway one of them ran, and took a spunge, and filled it with vinegar, and put it on *a reed, and gave him to drink. The rest said, Let be, let us see whether Elias will come to save him. Jesus, when he had cried again with a loud voice, yielded up the ghost. And, behold, the veil of the temple was rent in twain from the top to the bottom; and the earth did quake, and the rocks rent; and the graves were opened; and many bodies of the saints which slept arose, and came out of the graves after his resurrection, and went into the holy city, and appeared unto many"* (Matthew 27:45-53).

This is the ordinance of the watches by which day and night are controlled.

"Thus saith the Lord, which giveth the sun for a light by day, and the ordinances of the moon and of the stars for a light by night, which divideth the sea when the waves thereof roar; The Lord of hosts is his name: If those ordinances depart from before me, saith the Lord, then the seed of Israel also shall cease from being a nation before me forever" (Jeremiah 31:35-36).

The Watchman works by these watches, what they tell him, and how they lead him when the heavens open. The watches set road maps for the earth to follow. They have a pull on the earth. Day and night are ruled by them. God said to Job: *"Hast thou commanded the morning since thy days; and caused the dayspring to know his place; that it might take hold of the ends of the earth, that the wicked might be shaken out of it?"* (Job 38:12-13).

Angels and men set the rules on earth at the command of God. However, Angels serve God's will in man's life to fulfill the reason God created him on earth.

POTENT HOUR FOR WATCHMEN

Every first hour of the watches is a potent hour for the watchman. The third (midnight 12-3 am) and the fourth (3-6 am) watch were the most used hour of prayer by Jesus. He would leave His disciples at midnight to the mountain and return in the morning.

By these, He ruled both day and night. The Watchmen must follow in His steps to engage in warfare at midnight watches in order to change times and seasons and to receive Heaven's secrets.

> *"Then was the secret revealed unto Daniel in a night vision. Then Daniel blessed the God of heaven. Daniel answered and said, Blessed be the name of God forever and ever: for wisdom and might are his: And he changeth the times and the seasons: he removeth kings, and setteth up kings: he giveth wisdom unto the wise, and knowledge to them that know understanding"* (Daniel 2:19-21).

Peter redefined the meaning of clean and unclean at the beginning of a watch when an Angel visited him and showed him Yahweh's heart for the Gentiles. He was met at his duty post as a Watchman during a watch. Paul, another watchman told his story of how God revealed His secret to him. He narrated:

> *"How that he was caught up into paradise, and heard unspeakable words, which it is not lawful for a man to utter"* (2 Corinthians 12:4).

Paul, John, and Peter can be equated to Ezekiel, Isaiah, and Jeremiah. They all had special missions that changed times and seasons. They rewrote history. What can we say of Philip whose daughters were all prophetesses? He was sent by the Holy Spirit to the Eunuch of Ethiopia who was on his way back to Ethiopia. That connection changed the history of Africa as he interpreted the secrets of Isaiah 53. It is now our time.

The Apostles were referred to as men who had turned "the world upside down." We must affect our generation the same way the Apostles and early disciples used the medium of watches to turn the world upside down for Christ.

Paul and other watchmen never spoke carelessly. Every word had a meaning so that,

> "To *the intent that now unto the principalities and powers in heavenly places might be known by the church the manifold wisdom of God"* (Ephesians 3:10).

The Watchman's tongue should always be bridled that when it opens, it brings forth fire and salvation. Let your words be seasoned that when you speak, deliverance takes place and men are saved.

TESTIMONIES & PICTORIALS

THE CARIBBEAN

Apostle Stephen Holford and New Dimensions Ministries was the one who opened the gates into Barbados for Apostle Dr. Emmanuel Nuhu Kure. This relationship blossomed into great meetings (including open-air meetings) and revivals (sometimes chaired by Apostle David Coulthrust) that affected the nation in ten years.

Apostle Ofodile Nzimiro caught a passion for the land while accompanying Dr. Kure. And within seven years prepared them for Jubilee that culminated into both Apostle Dr. Emmanuel Nuhu Kure and Apostle Chuck Pierce holding a great jubilee meeting in 2016.

The meeting attracted key ministers in the nation who joined to call forth the winds of change and progress. Minister Sonia Johnson became a central pivot for most of those meetings along with her ministry leadership later, summarizes the 2016 meeting thus:

WATCHMEN TESTIFIES OF BARBADOS JUBILEE 2016

Apostle Ofodile Nzimiro had prepared the nation for seven years through constant teachings and prophetic action.

The year 2016 finally came; it was our nation's Jubilee year and we looked forward to all that God had promised. According to Leviticus 25: 811, we obeyed our God instructions and planned our jubilee celebration beginning June 7, 2016.

Before the celebration, our Jubilee March started from New Dimensions Ministries into the city of Bridgetown where we prayed and had 50 flags waving the scripture blessings and having the ram horns sound as we sang out praises of thanksgiving to God.

By this time, with great excitement, we awaited the presence of Jehovah God. Our two invited Fathers of the faith, senior watchmen, led us in the celebrations; Apostle Emmanuel Kure and Apostle Chuck Pierce, not forgetting our beloved teacher, Apostle Ofodile Nzimiro.

A prophetic word was then given to the Nation by Apostle Chuck Pierce. He said that Barbados had to come into the structure that God intended for us.

As a nation, we were strategically positioned in our geographical location to display God's Kingdom power. Apostle Chuck Pierce stated that God's apostolic strength was upon our nation and that we were placed in conflict to develop a new identity, a new authority, a new atmosphere and gain the strategy that was necessary to secure our future.

We were advised that part of our destiny was to control the winds and that a sign of a great wind was coming for the nation but the wind was going to split into two and go around the nation. His final words to us were, "Barbados will rise".

These words were the beginning of the great spiritual explosion of the Holy Spirit's power in our meetings. Apostle Emmanuel Kure, our main guest speaker, led the celebrations namely in the capital of Barbados.

During the first two nights, we were blessed to have a representation of all our sectors, in the land including the government officials. Apostle Emmanuel Kure took a set of eleven stones from our seas which represented our eleven parishes.

He then called Senior Apostle Stephen Holford, representing the Church, Government Officials, The Honorable Patrick Todd, representing the Government and The Honorable Mia Amor Mottley representing the Opposition, the Honorable Michael Carrington, the Speaker of the House of Assembly, to all stand on the altar.

Apostle Kure invited them to raise a prayer for Barbados and its people, for having both Government and the Opposition party present marked the balance that was needed to help shift the nation back to its destiny. This symbolic prophetic action, even as he placed the Speaker of the House of Assembly with his gavel seated before the people, marked an eternal seal that would long be remembered.

We followed the Biblical pattern and God broke the yolk and opened the gates to our prosperous future. God was reconciling lives and the destiny of Barbados to His eternal purpose.

This very strategic action of the Lord had the Honorable Mia Mottley and the Honorable Patrick Todd praying for the nation as they both raised a cry for unity. The Opposition Leader also asked God to help us create the best and come together even when we face the worst. Apostle Stephen Holford prayed for the soul of the nation and sealed the prayer.

Apostle Emmanuel Kure prepared us for what was about to happen. Before he anointed the stones, Apostle Kure assured us that God was about to visit our foundations. He prayed for our season of restoration, for our character, our behavior and our patterns of life were about to be changed by our maker.

The stones bearing witness for Barbados, its people, its struggles, and its history were now about to witness another historic event. Apostle Kure prophesied that there was going to be a shift and a change in our politics, in our economy, in the orientation of our parliament for the good of the land.

He asked God to cut all kinds of slavery and as he anointed the stones, he declared three promises to the people, we shall become the praise of God in the earth, nothing shall shut down our progress, and that we were going to be clothed with God's blessings. On the voice of Amen, the Speaker of the House brought down the gavel to the sound of Jubilation from the people.

These nights of Jubilee celebrations continued in God. One of the highlights was the prophetic word given by Apostle Emmanuel Kure concerning the then opposition leader, the Honorable Mia Amor

Mottley who today is living in prophecy. She became the Prime Minister of the Nation.

Apostle Dr. Kure prophesied to the present Bajan (Barbados) Prime Minister, Hon. Mia Amor Mottley, that kingship was in her Bloodline from Africa. She became the next Prime Minister of Barbados.

Another significant highlight was the night when God strategically displayed and anointed the families. As Apostle Kure prayed, God began to visit our roots and dig us out of the shadows, releasing us into new spiritual garments.

On that same night, Apostle Kure prophesied that champions would arise from our nation, for we were not created to be ordinary but to be creators. He also prophesied that very precious stones will be discovered in our ocean and the glory of the seas would begin to cover our people. Apostle

Ofodile Nzimiro also shared encouraging Barbados to Arise.

As we approached the last day of our Jubilee celebration, it was clear to all who understood the mystery and revelation of Jubilee that Barbados was now ready to enter its new season. God had stirred a new awareness of His covenant plans to the land.

Testimonies had already started to be revealed. We were all ready and anxiously waiting for the revelation and manifestation of the Holy Spirit that will set the course of individuals, our people, and our nation.

The Great Encounter of the presence of God was about to happen. The evening started with joyous praise and worship. The blowing of the shofars invited all of creation and hearing the sweet worship of the saints was awesome, with their voices filling every section of the city.

People everywhere were expectant and by the time the worship was finished, the Holy Spirit had already stamped His authority and approval on the proceedings, bringing a Holy excitement to the atmosphere.

The Sunday evening Jubilee service held in Independence Square to climax our Jubilee celebrations was nothing less than glorious. From the raised altar, Apostle Emmanuel Kure's voice was heard sharing the seriousness of the Lord's Jubilee in our Nation and what was promised to us from Heaven.

Much deliverance to the people and the land was beseeched, many prayers were offered, many covenants were made as the sound of liberty was released over the city.

As Apostle Emmanuel Kure raised the staff of authority, many declarations were pronounced over Barbados, for the gates of our Lord were opened unto us and nothing coming to our shores will destroy us.

Today even in the COVID-19 pandemic, Barbados was one of the nations that left its borders opened to be a solution to many and an olive branch to the weak and helpless.

The event was monumental as Apostle Kure called all the many Pastors to stand facing the land and the people. The Elders of 50-and-over years old faced the altar while the people took something natural from the land.

The children joined him on the altar and together we lifted our hands and voices to the heavens and called on the Creator of Heaven and Earth, the Ancient of Days, to set His throne in Barbados. It was an incredible experience and a phenomenal happening that we will never forget. God's divine presence came over our city, our land, over the sea, and our people.

As Apostle Kure said the Spirit of Jubilee would not end with these celebrations but would continue and live on in our Nation. And today, we watch our nation realigned to the prophecies and the promises of our God.

We see the unity emerging among our people under the leadership of our Prime Minister, the Honorable Mia Amor Mottley. We see our economy building a future for our people and we see a nation whose God is the Lord.

The Jubilee celebrations that evening closed with a people whose hearts were glad as we joyfully made music and danced and praised God for fulfilling all His promises.

Apostle David Coulthrust of Nation of Worship Global commented among other things that I wondered whether I should vividly recount how he spoke with passion as a prophetic watchman to the pastors of this nation, regarding the prophetic destiny of Barbados and its place in the spirit, as well as the importance of our Jubilee.

He was sounding the alarm of heaven, commanding the pastors to arise and defend the nation; to use Jubilee to reset the foundations of a nation which was in bondage, but which God desperately wanted to release.

Certainly more than a passing word should be dedicated to telling of his prophesy over our church (Nation Of Worship) regarding the acquisition of land that has come to pass; to his generosity to us which transformed our impact as a ministry and to the wise counsel which he gave to me personally regarding ministry and how to truly identify sons and daughters in the spirit. This has shaped me and my ministry in ways that are too numerous to mention.

Time will not allow me to speak of the generational curses which have been broken over this nation forever, by the depth of revelation which flowed like a river from Apostle Kure; regarding the spiritual realm, of how to pray and how to contend for God's will over our lives and our nation. Now we can no longer be destroyed because we lack knowledge.

From the example of how he raised, mentored, and released his son Apostle Ofodile Nzimiro who continues his work amongst us; to the powerful ministry of his anointed wife Pastor Martha Kure, who has also impacted this nation; much can be said about this man of God. The mark of a true apostle is reflected in those that they raise and release.

The oil on his head is powerfully manifested in his beloved spiritual son and his wonderful wife. They have continued to service and build upon the foundational altars that he has established in this nation each time they visit Barbados.

Let it be known that when the story of Barbados' glory is told in heaven one day when the story of its rise is trumpeted amongst the host of heaven,

Apostle Kure's name will be amongst those that heaven rewards for setting a nation free and building new foundations.

God Bless you, Son of Heaven, you are marked for favor. As long as there is a place called Barbados on the earth, your generations will never cease to be blessed. Your name is written in our foundations for the good of this nation.

The Barbados Meeting.

RENAISSANCE - GHANA & SENEGAL

For two years (2009 – 2010) Apostle Dr. Emmanuel Nuhu Kure brought people from the Caribbean and black Americans from the US to connect with their roots and break hindrances in their various nations related to their roots. Prophetess Melissa Simon of the Restore Your Crown Centre, St. John's, Antigua and Barbuda summarized the trips thus:

The earth is the Lords and the fullness, therefore, is the foundation I believe we all ventured to accept the invitation of Apostle Emmanuel Kure to visit the slave trade routes in both Ghana and Senegal. It is now almost 11 years and most of the experiences resound in our memory with the mixed emotions we felt on the pilgrimages.

In March of 2008, Apostle Emmanuel Nuhu Kure and his wife Pastor Martha Kure landed in Antigua to spend two days before moving to the neighboring island of Montserrat under the patronage of Former Ambassador Lauren Fenton. It is coincidental, I am writing this review as I was the one seconded to meet and greet Apostle and Pastor Kure on behalf of Apostle Stephen Andrews and SJPC House of Restoration.

Two nights of services were scheduled and the body of Christ was invited. The tabernacle was packed with many in high expectations as to what a man of God from Africa has to reveal. The teachings were mind-blowing and to say the least, we never saw such revelations, enlightenment, and more so scriptures.

To add, the prophetic actions seemed like a drama. Apostle Kure opened the scroll of prophetic actions with anointing oil and salt like in 2 Kings 2:20, after this experience we used salt and oil at every prayer. Early morning prayer before 6am was never practiced but Apostle Andrews and later many other ministries started holding such meetings with great testimonies of healing as we united to petition heaven at the womb of the morning.

I recall clearly at one of the meetings we were told to bring artifacts of books and other items from the demonic world and two barrels were brought to burn them, the red smoke that emerged was an assurance that deliverances were secured.

Apostle Emmanuel and Pastor Martha Kure along with Apostle Ofodile Nzimiro returned in 2009 for another conference, along with a final visit in 2011 to dedicate the New 2500 seater sanctuary for Apostle Andrews. This visit showed us how to prophetically open the gates with dedication prayers starting outside the building, and long abolishing the cutting of the ribbon to dedicate a building but smearing the lintels and doorposts which we use until now to put the mark of the presence of God.

It was also at this time we understood interpretations of dreams, warfare prayers calling for hunters, fishers, flying scroll, etc., which we followed from the book "Practical Prophetic Prayers by Apostle Emmanuel Nuhu Kure".

It was based on these encounters and testimonies from a pioneering watchman Apostle, that a team of 16 persons from Antigua, St. Lucia, and Trinidad went to Ghana and Senegal for the slave trade and then to Nigeria for the International Prophetic Prayers Conference.

I recall in Ghana the tour exposed the life of slaves and it was an emotional time as we imagined ourselves being squashed into a small room, limited and no food, and women suffering the humiliation. It was on one of these visits we saw the door of NO RETURN and we felt the freedom as Apostle Kure prayed a prayer of release.

On this tour, we took communion at the gates of time in Ghana which is connected in Barbados. A planned church service was emotional as the presence of Portuguese Americans kneeled to apologize to the Africans and the Africans kneeled to apologize to us the Caribbean.

We prayed and accepted the apology although many of us were confused and ignorant of our history and so was very grateful for Apostle Kure for this invitation. An offering was collected as a ransom, again we did not know about the ransom offer but felt a deep release.

Senegal's experience was shorter although visiting the slave sites (Goree Island) with similar stories as in Ghana brought further enlightenment. In Senegal, we were taken on a boat ride to experience the journey and bought souvenirs to seal the memory and experience.

Part of the team from the Caribbean – Antigua, St. Lucia, and Montserrat, led by Apostle Stephen Andrews (Antigua) and Ambassador Lauren Fenton (Montserrat). The Bajans were also on this trip – 2009.

In brief, the Caribbean has never been the same since the visit and relationship which was coined by Apostle Emmanuel Kure and Throneroom

Trust Ministry. One of Throneroom's visions is to raise Priests and dotted around the Caribbean there and many who bears the mark of the watchman anointing that Apostle Kure released.

The significant difference is that many from the western world come with words and no manifestations but when you see barrenness turned to fruitfulness, insomnia healed, weddings, blossoming of businesses; it is undeniable that the grace upon Apostle Kure brought breakthroughs by his sound teachings. We salute a stalwart, and I urge us to read the many books to get a deeper revelation of the truth of prophetic prayers.

The Team at Elmina Castle (Cape Coast),
Ghana led by a Tour Guide

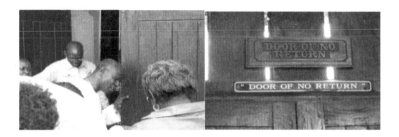

Apostle Kure prophesying at the Door of No
Return – Elmina Castle, Ghana

Praying at Slave River and Ancestral River Park
where slaves took their Last Bath – Ghana

Dr. Marilyn, Apostle Kure, Fe Hester and Ginger Cantrell aka
Mama Throneroom – USA in Tema, Ghana

Communion at the Prime Meridian Shoreline – Tema,
Ghana with Caribbean and American team. Breaking the
yoke of time and the curse of slavery over the nations.
Prophet Kure and the stones of Time - Tema, Ghana

GOREE ISLAND – SENEGAL

The Boat Ride to Goree Island Senegal - Prayers on the waters.

*Apostle Kure with Apostle Stephen Andrews at
Goree Island Museum, Senegal*

The Team at Goree Island, Senegal

PART TWO

DANIEL 5:11-12

> *There is a man in thy kingdom, in whom is the spirit of the holy gods; and in the days of thy father light and understanding and wisdom, like the wisdom of the gods, was found in him; whom the king Nebuchadnezzar thy father, the king, I say, thy father, made master of the magicians, astrologers, Chaldeans, and soothsayers; Forasmuch as an excellent spirit, and knowledge, and understanding, interpreting of dreams, and shewing of hard sentences, and dissolving of doubts, were found in the*

same Daniel, whom the king named Belteshazzar: now let Daniel be called, and he will shew the interpretation.”

11

An Overview of the Watchman

THE WATCHMAN AND THE LAND

W atchmen are redeemers of the land. They release the land from satanic covenants, desecrations through bloodshed from war, and other practices contrary to God's will. The Bible says,

"Don't desecrate the land in which you live. I live here too — I, GOD, live in the same neighborhood with the People of Israel" (Numbers 35:34, MSG).

Leviticus 25:24 says, "You must provide for the right of redemption for any of the land that you own" (MSG).

Watchmen help the land keep her Sabbaths unto the Lord.

> *"To fulfill the word of the LORD by the mouth of Jeremiah, until the land had enjoyed her sabbaths: for as long as she lay desolate she kept sabbath, to fulfill threescore and ten years"* (2 Chronicles 36:21, KJV).

According to Jewish tradition, the land is supposed to be left fallow and unfarmed for one year after every seven years to allow it to renew itself and be renewed by the dew of heaven. The land is supposed to be granted rest.

The Watchman fights for the natural preservation of the land. He understands the natural and spiritual rules binding land and nature and ensures that these rules are kept. He helps the land keep the rules of God from time to time according to the dictates of God.

He causes time to change according to the dispensation of the will of the Lord as he sees it in the spirit realm and from the Word. He controls and influences seasons by praise, intercession, and prophetic actions.

He carries out prophetic actions to change the course of events and seasons. Ezekiel 4:4-6 says:

> *"Lie thou also upon thy left side, and lay the iniquity of the house of Israel upon it: according to the number of the days that thou shalt lie upon it thou shalt bear their iniquity. For I have laid upon thee the years of their iniquity, according to the number of the days, three hundred and ninety days: so shalt thou bear the iniquity of the house of Israel. And when thou hast accomplished them, lie again on thy right side, and thou shalt bear the iniquity of the house of Judah forty days: I have appointed thee each day for a year."*

For 390 days, Ezekiel, literally, laid down against the sins of Israel, and another 40 days for Judah to weigh upon them the punishment that Yahweh has placed upon them. His obedience caused the watchers in charge of times and seasons to act according to the implication of what he physically enacted.

The Watchman is a medium of God's transmissions on earth. God cannot transmit punishment or blessing on earth except He passes through a man. God created the earth for man to rule; it is the ruler that transmits change. The Watchman, therefore, is a prophetic ruler used by God to cause a change on earth.

Prophetic physical actions transmit that rule of God. It releases heaven to act because the gatekeeper ruler has opened the door.

THE EFFECT OF PROPHETIC ACTIONS

Prophetic words and actions created Nebuchadnezzar and changed the course of history. Jeremiah 43:9-12 says,

> "Take great stones in thine hand, and hide them in the clay in the brickkiln, which is at the entry of Pharaoh's house in Tahpanhes, in the sight of the men of Judah; And say unto them, "Thus saith the LORD of hosts, the God of Israel; Behold, I will send and take Nebuchadrezzar the king of Babylon, my servant, and will set his throne upon these stones that I have hid; and he shall spread his royal pavilion over them. And when he cometh, he shall smite the land of Egypt, and deliver such as are for death to death; and such as are for captivity to captivity; and such as are for the sword to the sword. And I will kindle a fire in the houses of the gods of Egypt; and he shall burn them, and carry them away captives: and he shall array himself with the land of Egypt, as a shepherd putteth on his garment; and

he shall go forth from thence in peace."

Isaiah carried out a prophetic action by walking naked for three years, as a sign of how God would make Egypt and Ethiopia walk bare buttocks for three years. God collaborates with man to rule the earth.

> *"At the same time spake the LORD by Isaiah the son of Amoz, saying, Go and loose the sackcloth from off thy loins, and put off thy shoe from thy foot. And he did so, walking naked and barefoot. And the LORD said, Like as my servant Isaiah hath walked naked and barefoot three years for a sign and wonder upon Egypt and upon Ethiopia; So shall the king of Assyria lead away the Egyptians prisoners, and the Ethiopians captives, young and old, naked and barefoot, even with their buttocks uncovered, to the shame of Egypt"* (Isaiah 20:2-4).

Watchmen work together with the Angels in Heaven to set boundaries for good and evil, crossing that set line attracts repercussions. Like the Angels, watchmen have measuring tapes.

> *"I looked up and was surprised to see a man holding a tape measure in his hand. I said, "What are you up to?" "I'm on my way," he said, "to survey Jerusalem, to measure its width and length." Just then the Messenger Angel on his way out met another angel coming in and said, "Run! Tell the Surveyor, 'Jerusalem will burst its walls — bursting with people, bursting with animals. And I'll be right there with her' — GOD's Decree — 'a wall of fire around unwalled Jerusalem and a radiant presence within'"* (Zechariah 2:1-5, MSG).

Some of these cannot be accomplished without a God-ordained fast accompanying.

> *"And he said unto them, This kind can come forth by nothing, but by prayer and fasting." (Mark 9:29)*

All you need is to discern the kind of sacrifice the Lord requires. Sometimes it is praise God wants, sometimes it is a fast, and other times it could be a prophetic action. You need to always discern what God wants.

THE GOAL OF WATCHMEN FOR THE LAND

"Violence will never again be heard of in your land; devastation and destruction will be gone from your borders. But you will name your walls Salvation, and your gates praise. The sun will no longer be your light by day, and the brightness of the moon will not shine on you; but the LORD *will be your everlasting light, and our God will be your splendor. Your sun will no longer set, and your moon will not fade; for the* LORD *will be your everlasting light, and the days of your sorrow will be over.   Then all your people will be righteous; they will possess the land forever; they are the branch I planted, the work of My hands, so that I may be glorified. The least will become a thousand, the smallest a mighty nation. I am the* LORD*; I will accomplish it quickly in its time"* (Isaiah 60:18-22).

Watchmen are needed in all the earth. Without them, God's program will not be fulfilled.

THE WATCHMAN AND GOD

The Watchman is the mouthpiece of God on the earth. He sees to it that prophecy is fulfilled. He worships God day and night and lives perpetually in the consciousness of God and His will. He abides under the shadow of the Almighty.

Watchmen love to WORSHIP, by which they create a perpetual habitation for God. They always make room for God. GOD FEEDS ON WORSHIP CUM FELLOWSHIP. Note that God dwells in the place of worship. His scriptural place of habitation is PRAISE, not prayer.

> *"But thou art holy, O thou that inhabitest the praises of Israel."*
> *(Psalm 22:3)*

Create a seat of worship for Him in your heart. Psalm 132:13 says,

> *"For the LORD hath chosen Zion; he hath desired it for his habitation."*

Exodus 15:2 says,

> *"The LORD is my strength and song, and he is become my salvation: he is my God, and I will prepare him an habitation; my father's God, and I will exalt him."*

THE GATEWAY TO HEAVEN

Always be in the spirit despite your physical vocations, callings, and gifts. Pray in the Holy

Ghost always. Develop it as a habit until it sticks. The Watchman sees beyond the physical realm because his spirit is always alive in prayer. The Watchman is the gateway to heaven. He keeps watch and sees things on earth as God sees them in Heaven.

> "*The watchman of Ephraim was with my God: but the prophet is a snare of a fowler in all his ways, and hatred in the house of his God*" (Hosea 9:8).

The Message translation of Hosea 9:8 says:

> "*The prophet is looking out for Ephraim, working under God's orders. But everyone is trying to trip him up. He's hated right in God's house, of all places.*"

THE WATCHMAN AND MAN

Watchmen guide men as recorded in Ezekiel 33:19. He clears the way for men to fulfill God-ordained destinies. The Bible says that they roll away stones of hindrance to open gates of destiny.

> "*Go through, go through the gates; prepare ye the way of the people; cast up, cast up the highway; gather out*

> *the stones; lift up a standard for the people"* (Isaiah 62:10).

Jeremiah 43:9-10 says;

> *"Take great stones in thine hand, and hide them in the clay in the brick kiln, which is at the entry of Pharaoh's house in Tahpanhes, in the sight of the men of Judah; and say unto them, Thus saith the LORD of hosts, the God of Israel; Behold, I will send and take Nebuchadnezzar the king of Babylon, my servant, and will set his throne upon these stones that I have hid; and he shall spread his royal pavilion over them."*

It was this prophetic word that enthroned Nebuchadnezzar and the dimensions of his reign as King of Babylon.

RIDERS AND HORSEMEN

Watchmen are referred to as RIDERS or HORSEMEN. They ride in pairs.

> *"Look, riders come— horsemen in pairs." And he answered, saying, "Babylon has fallen, has fallen. All the idols of her gods have been shattered on the ground." My downtrodden and threshed people, I*

> *have declared to you what I have heard from the* LORD *of Hosts, the God of Israel"* (Isaiah 21:910, HCSB).

Prophet Isaiah emphasized and proclaimed the fall of Babylon. Sometimes, deep mystic nations like Babylon need a repeated prophecy to destroy her stronghold. Prophesying in pairs causes foundations to shift to fulfill God's will. The pair stands for a spiritual governmental agreement. Some destinies will not move except they hear the voices of deep spirited men prophesying at the same time.

It took the prophecies of many prophets to make Saul, a man, the first king in Israel. Deep had to speak to the deep. Watchmen must operate like prophets sent to redeem their nations and peculiar individuals.

Many prophets kept prophesying at Babylon including Apostle John, to see to both its spiritual and physical fall. Watchmen must continue to tarry until the promises of God are fulfilled on earth. We need watchmen who will open and shut the heavens as often as God wills until the kingdoms of this world become the kingdoms of our God. Where are His riders and horsemen among us?

The watchman activates family destinies and restores generational blessings.

"And they sung a new song, saying, Thou art worthy to take the book, and to open the seals thereof: for thou wast slain, and hast redeemed us to God by thy blood out of every kindred, and tongue, and people, and nation" (Revelation 5:9).

"Again, Jesse made seven of his sons to pass before Samuel. And Samuel said unto Jesse, The LORD hath not chosen these. And Samuel said unto Jesse, Are here all thy children? And he said, There remaineth yet the youngest, and, behold, he keepeth the sheep. And Samuel said unto Jesse, Send and fetch him: for we will not sit down till he come hither. And he sent, and brought him in. Now he was ruddy, and withal of a beautiful countenance, and goodly to look to. And the LORD said, Arise, anoint him: for this is he. Then Samuel took the horn of oil, and anointed him in the midst of his brethren: and the Spirit of the LORD came upon David from that day forward. So Samuel rose up, and went to Ramah" (1 Samuel 16:10-13).

"He gave Himself for us to redeem us from all lawlessness and to cleanse

*for Himself a special people, eager to
do good works"* (Titus 2:14, HCSB)

Finally, a major function of the Watchman is to
expose and lift the veil of false prophets.

*"Thus saith the Lord GOD; Behold, I
am against the shepherds; and I will
require my flock at their hand, and
cause them to cease from feeding the
flock; neither shall the shepherds feed
themselves any more; for I will deliver
my flock from their mouth, that they
may not be meat for them." (Ezekiel
34:10)*

We need forerunners of the end time who will
prepare the way for Angels to ride with us on
earth. It is time to join the company of the
heavenly hosts of Watchmen.

THE WATCHMAN AND THE HOLY SPIRIT

The Holy Spirit is the Transporter. He carries him
from the lock of his head from place to place in
visions, dreams, and out of body experience to
show him things and give an understanding of
the Father's heart. The Holy Spirit always travels
with the Watchman. The Watchman manifests in
the oil, presence, and the two-edged sword of God
in his mouth. These three are the greatest tools
God is using to tame the complex forces of

darkness that are coming against the Church in this end time (2 Thessalonians 2:8; Revelation 2:13-14).

The two-edged sword in the mouth of a watchman operates against Satan and his agents.

> *"And then shall that Wicked be revealed, whom the Lord shall consume with the spirit of his mouth, and shall destroy with the brightness of his coming"* (2 Thessalonians 2:8).

> *"Write this to Pergamum, to the Angel of the church. The One with the sharp biting sword draws from the sheath of his mouth — out come the sword words: "I see where you live, right under the shadow of Satan's throne. But you continue boldly in my Name; you never once denied my Name, even when the pressure was worst, when they martyred Antipas, my witness who stayed faithful to me on Satan's turf. "But why do you indulge that Balaam crowd? Don't you remember that Balaam was an enemy agent, seducing Balak and sabotaging Israel's holy pilgrimage by throwing unholy parties? And why do you put up with the Nicolaitans, who do the same thing? "Enough! Don't*

give in to them; I'll be with you soon.
I'm fed up and about to cut them to
pieces with my sword-sharp words"
(Revelation 2:12-16, MSG).

"Sword-sharp words" released from the place of friendship with the Holy Spirit will destroy the principalities of the air and their constellations that are being released in the air at this time. Their spells will be swayed and limited by words – "sword-sharp" Holy Ghost words!

The Holy Spirit for the watchman is about friendship with God. The Holy Spirit is his senior partner. He does not hide anything from the Watchman but reveals unto him the secret things of God.

> *"Howbeit when he, the Spirit of truth,*
> *is come, he will guide you into all truth:*
> *for he shall not speak of himself; but*
> *whatsoever he shall hear, that shall*
> *he speak: and he will shew you things*
> *to come." (John 16:13)*

He speaks in confidentiality and trust. Abraham as a friend of God had the privilege to negotiate for his cousin's life with God. The watchman also has the same privilege of negotiating and interceding with God for the safety of his people and nation. To prove His friendship with Abraham, God indulged him. Only friends indulge in such informalities. This is the relationship that exists between the Holy Spirit and the Watchman.

A FRIEND OF THE HOLY SPIRIT

> *"I do not call you slaves anymore, because a slave doesn't know what his master is doing. I have called you friends, because I have made known to you everything I have heard from My Father"* (John 15:15, HCSB).

The Watchman cultivates his friendship with the Holy Spirit. God relates with the watchman more like a partner than a friend. Until the Father accepts you as a friend, He will not reveal Himself. In this same vein, if a Watchman grieves the Holy Spirit, he becomes a stranger until he repents.

John, in the Book of Revelations, enjoyed the privileges of being in the Spirit and hearing the voice of God.

> *"I was in the Spirit on the Lord's day, and heard behind me a great voice, as of a trumpet"* (Revelation 1:10).

If you are reading this, begin to cultivate Him until He starts a "lock" relationship with you as He did with Ezekiel, carrying him to places. John in the book of Revelations enjoyed these privileges. Paul also.

The Lord led them John and Paul, the Apostles, into His audience because of the relationship. You need to transcend to that realm of a relationship if you must make impart on earth.

The Holy Spirit is the Chief Watchman. He dwells with us on earth as the eyes of the Father watching over us. He is the Watchman of the watchmen. The Holy Spirit sees everything, enters everywhere, and fills every vacuum. He sits in the high place and is found in the secret places where darkness and light meet – Genesis 1:2. Who else can be a better guide or arm of the watchman than the Third Person of the Godhead in the Trinity – the Holy Spirit. 2 Thessalonians 2:7-8 describes the Holy Spirit thus:

> *"For the mystery of iniquity doth already work: only he who now letteth will let, until he be taken out of the way. And then shall that Wicked be revealed, whom the Lord shall consume with the spirit of his mouth, and shall destroy with the brightness of his coming."*

The Holy Spirit defines the roles of the watchman if the watchman would listen. He brings him to the place of His watch and guides him to all that

He must do. The watchman does not at any point represent himself. He always represents the Holy Spirit and the will of the Father.

THE WATCHMAN AND THE FALLEN

Watchmen expose the Fallen and release the appointed. The fallen are demons that fell from the time of Noah and started a generation of "giants" among men. They only grieve God and increase sin. The fallen is Lucifer, who was cast out from Heaven along with his "angels" into the earth. The fallen and their agents torment the nations and distort destinies day and night; they are men who carry the doctrines of Balaam, Jezebel, and the Nicolaitans to the Church. They mix freely with Christians and destroy the testimony of the Church from within (Rev. 2:14, 15, 20). They also weaken and distort the image of the true and living God, turning Him into a liar.

Romans 1:21-23 says;

> *"Because that, when they knew God, they glorified him not as God, neither were thankful; but became vain in their imaginations, and their foolish heart was darkened. Professing themselves to be wise, they became fools, And changed the glory of the incorruptible God into an image made*

like to corruptible man, and to birds,
and four-footed beasts, and creeping
things."

The Fallen are kings (economic and political) who serve their (Fallen) purpose until God intervenes. These are the Fallen.

The Fallen lastly are fresh recruits – on whom spells are cast and are seduced on daily basis to do Satan's will in the short term or momentarily, discarding them after they have been used. For these ones, except they find Jesus and make Him Lord of their lives, they are lost forever. A wandering spirit possesses them after they have been used, never accomplishing anything or settling down. Going in circles all their lives become their lifestyle. Finding themselves tossed from pillar to post by circumstances till they die. It is these that are referred to in Jude 11-12.

"Woe unto them! for they have gone in
the way of Cain, and ran greedily
after the error of Balaam for reward,
and perished in the gainsaying of
Core. These are spots in your feasts
of charity, when they feast with you,
feeding themselves without fear:
clouds they are without water, carried

> *about of winds; trees whose fruit withereth, without fruit, twice dead, plucked up by the roots"* (Jude 11-12)

THE RAGING WAVES

Tainted "believers" and unbelievers are referred to as "raging waves" and "wandering stars," whom the Fallen have affected. Their destinies remain tainted except they repent and are delivered.

> *"Raging waves of the sea, foaming out their own shame; wandering stars, to whom is reserved the blackness of darkness forever"* (Jude 13).

It is the Watchman's business to sift and discern such people and save them from aborting God's purpose in their lives. They slow down or abort any of God's programs in their hands because they are "tainted."

In the pursuit of exposing Satan, Isaiah and Ezekiel were the greatest practical Biblical examples of watchmen. They spent their whole lives revealing God to men and EXPOSING SATAN and his wicked plans.

It was Isaiah who first exposed Satan as "Fallen." The first work of the Watchman, therefore, is to EXPOSE the vulnerability and reality of SATAN,

HELL, and DESTRUCTION which have kept people in fear.

Isaiah 14:12 says,

> *"How art thou fallen from heaven, O Lucifer, son of the morning! How art thou cut down to the ground, which didst weaken the nations!"*

Isaiah calls Satan a "Fallen." Ezekiel tells us what Satan is composed of and his present state as a Fallen.

> *"Thou art the anointed cherub that covereth; and I have set thee so: thou wast upon the holy mountain of God; thou hast walked up and down in the midst of the stones of fire. Thou wast perfect in thy ways from the day that thou wast created, till iniquity was found in thee. By the multitude of thy merchandise, they have filled the midst of thee with violence, and thou hast sinned: therefore I will cast thee as profane out of the mountain of God: and I will destroy thee, O covering cherub, from the midst of the stones of fire. Thine heart was lifted up because of thy beauty, thou hast corrupted thy wisdom by reason of thy brightness: I will cast thee to the*

*ground, I will lay thee before kings,
that they may behold thee. Thou hast
defiled thy sanctuaries by the
multitude of thine iniquities, by the
iniquity of thy traffick; therefore will I
bring forth a fire from the midst of
thee, it shall devour thee, and I will
bring thee to ashes upon the earth in
the sight of all them that behold thee"*
(Ezekiel 24:14-18).

Job shows that hell and destruction are the two
instruments that Satan and all the fallen use to
terrorize men. That these two instruments have
no powers of their own to harm except that which
is allowed them by YAHWEH for His glory.

*"The departed spirits tremble beneath
the waters and all that inhabit them.
Sheol is naked before God, and
Abaddon has no covering"* (Job 26:5-6,
HCSB).

The King James Version of the Above Bible
passage says:

*"Dead things are formed from under
the waters, and the inhabitants
thereof. Hell is naked before him, and
destruction hath no covering"* (Job
26:5-6, KJV).

It is the work of the Watchman to lay bare and demystify the hidden works of darkness that stand between God and man. The Watchman brings healing and restoration to the broken, frightened, and confused world. He helps the world to go through her rubbles and clean them up. He makes both darkness and light to fulfill their appointed divine purposes on earth in time.

All of God's Angels respond ONLY to God's will, while the fallen respond only to rituals and enchantments. The purpose of occultic powers is to imitate God's will and run a parallel government to God's. They disguise as being friendly but they work to satisfy man's desires and not God's will first.

ISSACHAR COMPANY OF WATCHMEN

The tribe of Issachar are watchmen. Of all the twelve tribes one whole tribe – Issachar – was made a Watchman tribe. God told me that it was the sacred tribe chosen to be the eyes of the Lord over Israel. They understand the times and know what Israel ought to do at every given time and season. No wonder they rode side by side with Judah to give him direction.

The Issachars were the advisers of Deborah. Without their counsel, she would not have won her battles against Barak. The tribe of Issachar joined hands with Heaven to win earth battles. The Holy Spirit in revelations told me that the Watchman is that tribe among us.

They lost the gift in time by failing to go to God to renew their strength. Israel had to go back to relying on seers and prophets like Ezekiel. Do not allow the wilderness to swallow your gift. Stay close and faithful to The Giver in order to remain His Eyes on earth.

God's will is for a tribe to watch over the other tribes.

> *"Hear another parable: There was a certain householder, which planted a vineyard, and hedged it round about, and digged a winepress in it, and* **BUILT A TOWER***, and let it out to husbandmen, and went into a far country"* (Matthew 21:33).

Notice that there must be a TOWER in a vineyard to watch over it.

Mark 12:1 says,

> *"And he began to speak unto them by parables. A certain man planted a vineyard, and set an hedge about it, and digged a place for the winefat,*

> and **BUILT A TOWER**, and let it out
> to husbandmen, and went into a far
> country."

A Tower enables a Watchman to watch over the
vineyard. The Kingdom of God is not complete
without them. The Kingdom of God cannot win
this last-day war without a tower and vineyard.
Are you part of that tribe? Answer the call and
take your place in conquest and dominion as the
eye and hand of the Lord. The tribe of Issachar
has been rebirthed in our days as WATCHMEN!

JOB AND AMOS

Job and Amos were accidental Watchmen. They
were dragged into spiritual warfare to expose how
heaven and earthworks and the real issues
between the spiritual and the physical. Only
Watchmen are given deep spiritual insights and
experiences like that. Ordinary men are "pawns"
in the hands of demons until they find and accept
the true God. John 17:3 says,

> "And this is life eternal, that they
> might know thee the only true God,
> and Jesus Christ, whom thou hast
> sent."

God used the plight of Job and Amos to tell their
story and expose revelations that would have
been hidden from men. Throughout the life of

Amos, he was uncomfortable with the idea of being a prophet. He wanted to be an ordinary herdsman (Amos 1:1; 7:15).

The Watchman, therefore, is a man of "excellent spirit and knowledge, and understanding, interpretation of dreams, showing of hard sentences and dissolving of doubts" whose aim is to make the world do the will of God at appointed times (Daniel 5:12).

The Muyiwa interview at Premier Radio preparatory to the London Prophetic Prayer Declarations on Brexit in Westminster Hall, London – April 2019

12

ZAMZUMMIMS

> *That also was accounted a land*
> *of giants: giants dwelt therein in*
> *old time; and the Ammonites call*
> *them Zamzummims." (Deut. 2:20)*

Zamzummims were sworn enemies of God. They opposed God's divine program in Israel and the earth. They were descendants of the sons of God, from the deity and roots of Ashtaroth in Hesbon.

> *"There were giants in the earth in*
> *those days; and also after that, when*
> *the sons of God came in unto the*
> *daughters of men, and they bare*
> *children to them, the same became*

*mighty men which were of old, men of
renown"* (Genesis 6:4-5).

The offsprings of Zamzummim are taking over the
earth. The fate of the world lies in the balance. It
is high time the Church and watchmen rose up to
face them.

ASHTAROTH

ASHTAROTH is the face of Satan in the
wilderness. It is the principality that rules in the
wilderness, even when Israel was going to the
Promised Land. These demonic power and
princes frustrated the leadership of Moses in the
wilderness and hindered him from entering into
Canaan.

Whenever the testimony of victory is given in the
wilderness, the most celebrated and the most
repeated, that even the Psalmist attributes to the
mercy of God, is the one against Og, King of
Bashan, and Ashtaroth. This is because the
secret power behind the path they were to follow
to their divine rest was ruled by Ashtaroth.

Moses conquered a lot of tribes in the wilderness
but only Sihon and Og are mentioned repeatedly
in the Books of Pentateuch, Joshua, and Psalm,
simply because they were the powers in charge of
the wilderness. In Psalms 136, no other king was

mentioned after Egypt except Sihon and Og of Ashtaroth. These kings were smitten by Jehovah Himself NOT Moses.

"O give thanks to the Lord of lords: for his mercy endureth forever. To him who alone doeth great wonders: for his mercy endureth forever. To him, that by wisdom made the heavens: for his mercy endureth forever. To him that stretched out the earth above the waters: for his mercy endureth forever. To him that made great lights: for his mercy endureth for ever: The sun to rule by day: for his mercy endureth for ever: The moon and stars to rule by night: for his mercy endureth forever. To him that smote Egypt in their firstborn: for his mercy endureth for ever: And brought out Israel from among them: for his mercy endureth for ever: With a strong hand, and with a stretched out arm: for his mercy endureth forever. To him which divided the Red sea into parts: for his mercy endureth for ever: And made Israel to pass through the midst of it: for his mercy endureth for ever: But overthrew Pharaoh and his host in the Red sea: for his mercy endureth forever. To him which led his people through the wilderness: for his mercy endureth for ever. To him which smote

great kings: for his mercy endureth for ever: And slew famous kings: for his mercy endureth for ever: Sihon king of the Amorites: for his mercy endureth for ever: And Og the king of Bashan: for his mercy endureth for ever: And gave their land for an heritage: for his mercy endureth for ever: Even an heritage unto Israel his servant: for his mercy endureth forever" (Psalms 136:3-22).

For God to go into the battle Himself against Ashtaroth shows the ignominity of the principalities involved. Historically, Ashtaroth is known as one of the gods of ancient times and served as such.

"And they forsook the Lord, and served Baal and Ashtaroth" (Judges 2:13).

1 Samuel 7:3, speaking of Ashtaroth, says:

"And Samuel spake unto all the house of Israel, saying, If ye do return unto the Lord with all your hearts, then put away the strange gods and Ashtaroth from among you, and prepare your hearts unto the Lord, and serve him only: and he will deliver you out of the hand of the Philistines."

Also 1 Samuel 31:10 says:

> *"And they put his armour in the house of Ashtaroth: and they fastened his body to the wall of Beth-shan."*

Sihon and Og kings were named after Ashtaroth and were characterized by extraordinary "seeds" called giants with six fingers and six toes. Their beds were nine cubits in length and four cubits in breadth apart from the weight and size of the arms they carried. Demons continued to sleep with daughters of men even after Noah's time and the flood. They still do in our day and are producing strange children in preparation for the reign of the Anti-Christ and Armageddon.

THE ANTICHRIST AND ARMAGEDDON

> *"Little children, it is the last time: and as ye have heard that antichrist shall come, even now are there many antichrists; whereby we know that it is the last time"* (1 John 2:18).

> *"For many deceivers are entered into the world, who confess not that Jesus Christ is come in the flesh. This is a deceiver and an antichrist"* (2 John 7).

And Revelation 16:16 says,

> *"And he gathered them together into a place called in the Hebrew tongue Armageddon."*

Note that the name of the major city and headquarters of these giants were dedicated to Ashtaroth. Ashtaroth gave life to these giants. It gave them thrones and platforms to work against God. Joshua 13:12 says,

> *"All the kingdom of Og in Bashan, which reigned in Ashtaroth and in Edrei, who remained of the remnant of the giants: for these did Moses smite, and cast them out by the ARM OF THE LORD."*

Apparently, these giants resurfaced in the wilderness to stand against God and His plans for His people on earth.

The Ashtaroth spirits in the human form shall play important roles in corrupting or trying to change times and seasons (Daniel 7). They will up the antenna against God and all that is right and good in nations. They will be governors and presidents, judges, traders, or even ordinary men waiting for their buttons to be pushed. Giants have characteristics of demonic DNA.

Unfortunately, these offspring of giants might be your next-door neighbors without you knowing, just waiting to be activated. The watchman will need to access that Arm of the Lord in Joshua to war against these spirits.

Joel 2 describes an army that will counter the influence of giants in the day of God's power.

> *"Behold, I will raise them out of the place whither ye have sold them, and will return your recompence upon your own head: And I will sell your sons and your daughters into the hand of the children of Judah, and they shall sell them to the Sabeans, to a people far off: for the Lord hath spoken it. Proclaim ye this among the Gentiles; Prepare war, wake up the mighty men, let all the men of war draw near; let them come up: Beat your plowshares into swords, and your pruninghooks into spears: let the weak say I am strong. Assemble yourselves, and come, all ye heathen, and gather yourselves together round about: thither cause thy mighty ones to come down, O Lord. Let the heathen be wakened, and come up to the valley of Jehoshaphat: for there will I sit to judge all the heathen*

roundabout. Put ye in the sickle, for the harvest is ripe: come, get you down; for the press is full, the fats overflow; for their wickedness is great" (Joel 3:7-13).

Where is that army? We must arise to build that army.

The spirit of prophecy is in travail to birth saviors, sons that will bring salvation to a world that has been blinded by the god of this world, the prince of the power of the air.

God is about to rouse an army that was once sold out and abused by Satan. God's Spirit is already moving in the deep waters and creating an army among those who were taken for granted, wounded, and counted as nothing. God will change your destiny and fortune overnight. He shall build systems that would swallow up the threat of these giants.

"But throughout the history of these kingdoms, the God of heaven will be building a kingdom that will never be destroyed, nor will this kingdom ever fall under the domination of another. In the end, it will crush the other kingdoms and finish them off and come through it all standing strong and eternal. It will be like the stone

> *cut from the mountain by the invisible hand that crushed the iron, the bronze, the ceramic, the silver, and the gold"* (Daniel 2:44-45, MSG).

God will give you wisdom, understanding, and knowledge to begin to create things without drawing attention to yourself. He will empower you with riches and influence to work signs and wonders. The army God shall raise through you shall be called the "tree of righteousness, the planting of the LORD."

Isaiah 61:3-4 says that God will

> *"...appoint unto them that mourn in Zion, to give unto them beauty for ashes, the oil of joy for mourning, the garment of praise for the spirit of heaviness; that they might be called trees of righteousness, the planting of the Lord, that he might be glorified. And they shall build the old wastes, they shall raise up the former desolations, and they shall repair the waste cities, the desolations of many generations."*

THE WEAK SHALL BE MADE STRONG

God will cause the weak to be strong for the task ahead. They will be dignified by the Holy Spirit and strengthened by the Almighty God. God speaking through Joel says,

> "*Beat your plowshares into swords, and your pruninghooks into spears: let the weak say, I am strong*" (Joel 3:10).

He will use the strength He created through you to draw them to the "valley of Jehoshaphat" (Joel 3:11-12) where He will expose and judge them. Their disguise has successfully fooled the world for a moment but interesting times are ahead because of the obedience of the saints.

ESTABLISHING GOD'S KINGDOM

The Watchmen will prophesy the following scriptures which will be useful while fighting the war against the kingdoms of the Zamzummims to establish God's Kingdom in the midst of their terror.

> "*Speak to Zerubbabel, governor of Judah, saying, I will shake the heavens and the earth; And I will overthrow the throne of kingdoms, and I will destroy the strength of the kingdoms of the heathen; and I will overthrow the chariots, and those that ride in them; and the horses and their riders shall come down, every one by*

the sword of his brother. In that day, saith the LORD of hosts, will I take thee, O Zerubbabel, my servant, the son of Shealtiel, saith the LORD, and will make thee as a signet: for I have chosen thee, saith the LORD of hosts" (Haggai 2:21-23).

"Seeing it is a righteous thing with God to recompense tribulation to them that trouble you;" (2 Thessalonians 1:6)

"And I will appoint over them four kinds, saith the LORD: the sword to slay, and the dogs to tear, and the fowls of the heaven, and the beasts of the earth, to devour and destroy" (Jeremiah 15:3).

"Cast forth lightning, and scatter them: Shoot out thine arrows, and destroy them" (Psalm 144:6).

"Break their teeth, O God, in their mouth: break out the great teeth of the young lions, O LORD" (Psalm 58:6).

"All nations compassed me about: but in the name of the LORD will I destroy them" (Psalm 118:10).

"The LORD preserveth all them that love him: but all the wicked will he destroy" (Psalm 145:20).

"And I will cut off witchcrafts out of thine hand; and thou shalt have no more soothsayers: Thy graven images also will I cut off, and thy standing images out of the midst of thee; and thou shalt no more worship the work of thine hands." (Micah 5:12-13)

"Then they will cry out to the LORD, but He will not answer them. He will hide His face from them at that time because of the crimes they have committed. This is what the LORD says concerning the prophets who lead my people astray, who proclaim peace when they have food to sink their teeth into but declare war against the one who puts nothing in their mouths. Therefore, it will be night for you— without visions; it will grow dark for you— without divination. The sun will set on these prophets, and the daylight will turn black over them." (Micah 3:4-6 HCSB)

"Thou shalt not suffer a witch to live." (Exodus 22:18)

"But these two things shall come to thee in a moment in one day, the loss of children, and widowhood: they shall come upon thee in their perfection for the multitude of thy sorceries, and for the great abundance of thine enchantments." (Isaiah 47:9)

"And I will come near to you to judgment; and I will be a swift witness against the sorcerers, and against the adulterers, and against false swearers, and against those that oppress the hireling in his wages, the widow, and the fatherless, and that turn aside the stranger from his right, and fear not me, saith the LORD of hosts." (Malachi 3:5)

"Yea, the light of the wicked shall be put out, and the spark of his fire shall not shine. His strength shall be hungerbitten, and destruction shall be ready at his side. It shall devour the strength of his skin: even the firstborn of death shall devour his strength. His roots shall be dried up beneath, and above shall his branch be cut off. His remembrance shall perish from the earth, and he shall have no name in the street. He shall

be driven from light into darkness, and chased out of the world." (Job 18:5, 12-13, 16-18)

"I saw the LORD *standing upon the altar: and he said, Smite the lintel of the door, that the posts may shake: and cut them in the head, all of them; and I will slay the last of them with the sword: he that fleeth of them shall not flee away, and he that escapeth of them shall not be delivered." (Amos 9:1)*

"And I will kill her children with death; and all the churches shall know that I am he which searcheth the reins and hearts: and I will give unto every one of you according to your works." (Revelations 2:23)

"And the earth helped the woman, and the earth opened her mouth, and swallowed up the flood which the dragon cast out of his mouth." (Revelations 12:16)

"Like sheep, they are laid in the grave; death shall feed on them; and the upright shall have dominion over them in the morning; and their beauty

shall consume in the grave from their dwelling." (Psalm 49:14)

"He shall flee from the iron weapon, and the bow of steel shall strike him through. It is drawn, and cometh out of the body; yea, the glittering sword cometh out of his gall: terrors are upon him. All darkness shall be hid in his secret places: a fire not blown shall consume him; it shall go ill with him that is left in his tabernacle. The heaven shall reveal his iniquity; and the earth shall rise up against him." (Job 20:24-27)

"But if the LORD make a new thing, and the earth open her mouth, and swallow them up, with all that appertain unto them, and they go down quick into the pit; then ye shall understand that these men have provoked the LORD." (Numbers 16:30)

"There shall the fire devour thee; the sword shall cut thee off, it shall eat thee up like the cankerworm: make thyself many as the cankerworm, make thyself many as the locusts." (Nahum 3:15)

"Wilt thou yet say before him that slayeth thee, I am God? but thou shalt be a man, and no God, in the hand of him that slayeth thee." (Ezekiel 28:9)

"Behold, I am against thee, saith the LORD *of hosts, and I will burn her chariots in the smoke, and the sword shall devour thy young lions: and I will cut off thy prey from the earth, and the voice of thy messengers shall no more be heard." (Nahum 2:13)*

"And it shall come to pass in that day, saith the LORD *of hosts, that I will cut off the names of the idols out of the land, and they shall no more be remembered: and also I will cause the prophets and the unclean spirit to pass out of the land." (Zechariah 13:2)*

"And the strong shall be as tow, and the maker of it as a spark, and they shall both burn together, and none shall quench them." (Isaiah 1:31)

"As birds flying, so will the LORD *of hosts defend Jerusalem; defending also he will deliver it; and passing over he will preserve it." (Isaiah 31:5)*
"Then they will cry out to the LORD*, but He will not answer them. He will hide His face from them at that time*

because of the crimes they have committed. This is what the LORD says concerning the prophets who lead my people astray, who proclaim peace when they have food to sink their teeth into but declare war against the one who puts nothing in their mouths. Therefore, it will be night for you— without visions; it will grow dark for you— without divination. The sun will set on these prophets, and the daylight will turn black over them."
(Micah 3:4-6 HCSB)

13

ANTI-CHRIST

The Anti-Christ is a product of the giants discussed in Chapter Eleven. He would not necessarily be a giant in the physique. But he shall come from the direct bloodline of the fallen demons.

Jesus is of the human bloodline of David. Before David began his ministry of public manifestation, he battled Goliath. The Messiah will have to face or battle with the Anti-Christ at his second coming. Goliath was of the bloodline of those giants, and the strange part is that he was a distant relation of David.

History has a way of churning out things the same way God closely monitors and makes creation to fulfill His will on earth. David's conquest of Goliath is a premonition of the Messiah in the loins of David who will destroy the Anti-Christ.

Have you ever wondered why Joab in 1 Chronicle 20 and 2 Samuel 12:26 refused to take Rabbah after seizing its waters but insisted that David takes the honor of conquest? That city defines Israel's destiny as a nation in God's program. It was the same city that Og, King of Bashan ruled from. The giants who resisted God in the wilderness established their headquarters there. It is therefore important that a person from the bloodline of the Messiah conquered it. The Church will have to face someday these GIANTS and she must be prepared to conquer them with the Word of God and the Blood of the Lamb.

The "Royal City" is a place where the fallen angels took human form to fight against God and man. It is a cauldron of Satan's pride and prowess on earth. Only those who are ordained of God can take that city. Joab knew this. That explains why he invited David from the bloodline of the Messiah, to take it. The battle of the end will be a power play that will pitch the Messiah against Satan's forces as recorded in Daniel 11:38:

"But in his estate shall he honor the God of forces: and a god whom his

fathers knew not shall he honor with gold, and silver, and with precious stones, and pleasant things."

In these last days, Angel Michael shall rise to fight for God's people as they pitch their battles against the ancient spirits.

"And at that time shall Michael stand up, the great prince which standeth for the children of thy people: and there shall be a time of trouble, such as never was since there was a nation even to that same time: and at that time thy people shall be delivered, every one that shall be found written in the book" (Daniel 12:1).

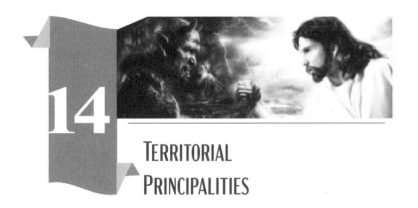

14

TERRITORIAL
PRINCIPALITIES

> **❝** *For we wrestle not against flesh and blood, but against principalities, against powers, against the rulers of the darkness of this world, against spiritual wickedness in high places"* (Ephesians 6:12).

Principalities have certain territories they control. Some move from place to place according to the demand for them by their masters. The believers are to keep their territories free of their influence, control, and manipulations. Like the Templars who kept the highways into Jerusalem free from thieves and marauders and protected the pilgrims who went to Jerusalem to pray.

Christians are to keep the spiritual highway and access to God free and open in the territories where He has placed them or wherever they find themselves for people to access and for Him to access His people with His blessings in the heavenly places.

The Watchman keeps the door open for Christians to access God freely. He protects communities from demonic habitations and ensures that no wayfaring demon settles permanently in his territory. The Watchman also opens the doorways of Heaven for the people to experience God in all ramifications of His glory by entering into His presence and habitation with praise. Teaching the people through the ministry and help of the Holy Spirit to love God and to serve Him according to the provision of the Holy scriptures. The Bible being the sole reference point.

FELLOWSHIP

Heaven and earth meet to fellowship with each other. The essence of life is fellowship. Fellowship between God and man, and between man and creation. Fellowship maintains peace and tranquillity in society and opens an atmosphere for creativity and growth in the world.

THE ROLES OF WATCHMEN IN FELLOWSHIP

The main role of the watchman is to keep the worship of God alive and the fulfillment of prophecies until the Messiah comes. The watchmen always stand between darkness and light on the earth, and ensures that the children of God on earth are kept safe.

Lastly and most importantly, the Watchmen plays the role of a heavenly judge. They tilt the scales of justice for the oppressed through prayer, spiritual travail, and decrees till the Messiah physically returns. They set boundaries against idols and the anti-Christ spirit, thereby maintaining territories by releasing God's spirit of jealousy to devour idols.

WATCHMEN AS SPIRITUAL JUDGES

As a spiritual judge, he makes way for the Master of all creation to rule according to the seasons ordained in Heaven. The Watchman finds his fulfillment and inheritance on earth when he rules and judges righteously. He locates the seat of Satan in every community, and either destroy it or makes it ineffective. He sits as a judge over territories. He does this by bringing the LIGHT OF GOD into the community. This is what makes a true watchman.

"As long as I am in the world, I am the light of the world." (John 9:5)

"And I will come near to you to judgment; and I will be a swift witness against the sorcerers, and against the adulterers, and against false swearers, and against those that oppress the hireling in his wages, the widow, and the fatherless, and that turn aside the stranger from his right, and fear not me, saith the LORD of hosts. For I am the LORD, I change not; therefore ye sons of Jacob are not consumed." (Malachi 3:5-6)

TESTIMONIES & PICTORIALS

ZAMBIA

DR. EMMANUEL NUHU KURE'S WORK IN ZAMBIA

Firstly, we want to thank Jehovah God that he always has a plan and a purpose for everything. The bible says God will not do anything except he reveals it to His prophets and when you believe his prophets, you will prosper and be established in that thing.

Zambia has not gone into any season without a word from the Lord. A word of warning, direction, guidance, and exhortation. Since early 2000, Dr. Kure has been part of Zambia's fabric. We have witnessed his sacrifice and commitment to the nation of Zambia. Dr. Kure has prophesied the many changes that Zambia has experienced in the economy, the church, the land, and its people and the politics of the nation of Zambia. He has helped the Church to interpret the seasons and given and given direction which has broken off her limitations and strategically positioned Zambia in redemptive purpose to begin to carry her banner for Christ.

For seven years, Dr. Kure helped the church through his teachings and prophecies to prepare for Jubilee.

1. Prayers were conducted in the major towns of Zambia to bring reconciliations and healings to the lands, rivers, and people of Zambia.
2. Seven Altars of peace were raised in the provinces.
3. A team was sent to the first capital city of Zambia in Kalomo to clean up the umbilical code that was raising an accusation because the people of Zambia had ignored it.

When there have been provocations from the enemy threatening to shift the roots and foundations of the nation of Zambia, Dr. Kure has stood with the nation through prayer and prophetic actions.

1. Marched through the streets of Lusaka from Cabinet Office through State House ending up in a crusade.
2. Gone to Kabwe and revealed the actual place at Mulungushi Rock of authority where Zambia's freedom fighters used to

meet and plan for Zambia's independence. A plaque has been put there to honor Jehovah God.

3. From this same rock of authority, stones were taken from it to be thrown in the major rivers of Zambia.

4. A team was sent to all the provinces of Zambia and on the same day of 7 March 2014, there was a pegging of the land.

5. On 23rd October 2014 the eve of Zambia's Jubilee, the Jubilee sound was released in the land of Zambia televised louder fireworks and in attendance was Zambia's new President who Dr. Kure had prophesied.

6. On 10th may, 2014, Dr. Kure on one of his sacrificial visits according to Leviticus 25, on the Zambian national broadcasting T.V station, televised on a live production for 3 hours of the blowing of the shofars to celebrate a jubilee. In attendance was former President Rupiah Banda, Pastor Vice president Nevers Mumba.

Dr. Kure at The Anglican Cathedral of The Holy Cross

In the Politics of Zambia, Dr. Kure has given a word which we have since seen came to pass.

In the year 2006, Dr. Kure at a meeting on the Copperbelt Province prophesied that the then sitting President would be re-elected when it looked very unlikely as an opposition leader was favored. He went on to prophesy that this President would not finish his term, he died (sadly this came to pass. The president didn't finish his term).

President Frederick Chiluba

President Levy P. Mwanawasa

President Rupiah Banda

President Michael Sata

President Edgar Lungu

During the course of President Rupiah Banda's term, Dr. Kure had an opportunity to meet him and gave him counsel about some of his Cabinet Ministers by name who were undermining him. Soon after that, we saw changes in his Cabinet appointment. Dr. Kure prophesied "a transition within a transition" where Zambia would get a President who was a short bridge on whose back the people of Zambia would cross. Despite the huge sums of money that were pumped in his election campaign President Banda only served 3 years and lost the election to President Sata to fulfill the word of God.

President Sata "Dubbed king cobra" came into power and started the massive infrastructure that Dr. Kure had prophesied about in Zambia. Without following usual procedure about budgets, like a madman, he started announcing the formations of new Districts which saw the development of new roads and buildings in forlorn townships and desolate places.

During the Jubilee preparations, Dr. Kure had prophesied about Zambia getting a Jubilee leader. In the natural, this could not be possible because we recently had elections in 2011 where president Sata had been elected President and he was in good health, and the environment in every sphere seemed to support his leadership which would only come up for re-election in 2015. The word of God is forever settled and will not return to Him void until it has fulfilled its purpose. In August 2014, President Sata died and a new Jubilee leader was ushered in Zambia by the name of President Edgar Lungu.

President Lungu is a midwife for all these developments. The next phase is a complex one. Zambia is due for another phase where the miracle of Zambia will begin to manifest the phase of her fullness, the fullness of her glory. Whether he can manage the next phase is the test. In this new calendar, Zambia must begin to shine out from her shadows. This president declared a National Day of Prayer, rededicated Zambia a Christian Nation, and decided to build God an
Altar.

THE CHURCH

When it comes to Zambia, God is forceful and not negotiable, because of its redemptive purpose. God made the nation of Zambia for his purpose and will not have the dragon to reign. In May 1873 in a village in Chitambo, David Livingstone prayer was "Lord on the land where I rest my bended knees Zambia, LET IT BECOME a Mighty CHRISTIAN NATION... A BEACON OF HOPE to the AFRICAN Continent and a light to the rest of the WORLD. President Fredrick Chiluba who Dr. Kure has met on 29th December 1991 entered the NATION OF ZAMBIA into a COVENANT WITH

GOD. God is maturing the church and the Church are the interpreters of the next program and will give the nation direction.

Dr. Kure has interacted and been invited to speak in many big and small churches in Zambia from the Catholics, Pentecostals, Anglican and United Church of Zambia. The prayer groups that have organized the meetings where he spoke were always inter-denominational.

Fr. Lupapa and Apostle Dr. Kure – Great Friends, Great Fires of the Spirit burning in Zambia. The last 15 years have seen great waves of the Holy Spirit.

Fr. Lupupa who was very close to President Sata was given instructions to carry out some prophetic actions at State House when there was a threat from the enemy. Dr. Kure has dedicated himself to God to ensure that he sees that God is maturing His church in Zambia.

In 2019 Throneroom Zambia was born. Through this vessel. Dr. Kure is raising watchmen to watch over the nation of Zambia.

Throneroom Zambia Board Members at the Inauguration Ceremony

Graduation Ceremony of students - Chief Chipepo is receiving his certificate from our Guest of Honour, Minister of Youth and Sport representing the Minister of Religious affairs.

In 2019, Dr. Kure had a 5 weeks Prayer and Legislation Prophetic School where 240 students were commissioned to arise to the clarion call of Jesus Christ and build him a formidable kingdom.

Dr. Kure's four daughters who are nicknamed "the four musketeers" who have labored in the Vineyard in Zambia.

Dr. Kure with Church Leaders and the Minister of Religious Affairs, Hon. Godfriday Sumaili in attendance.

Dr. Kure with the Hon Godfridah Sumaili - Minister of
Religious Affairs with the Board Chairman - Throneroom
Zambia, Dr. Roland Msiska.

ZIMBABWE

Prophet Dr. Emmanuel Nuhu Kure ministering at the
Jubilee Christian Centre, Lezard Avenue, Milton Park,
Harare, Zimbabwe

Broken Pots of Oppression Over the Nation of Zimbabwe

Zimbabwe Debts Cancelled.

Not long after this meeting, the memorable bloodless removal of President Robert Mugabe took place.

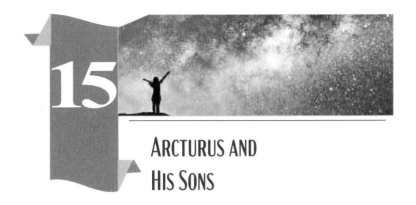

15

ARCTURUS AND
HIS SONS

T he sons of Arcturus were to confront the offsprings of giants, at the cry of the saints and watchmen who groan and watch with a desire for the coming of the Messiah. It will be in answer to their "demand" that the constellations and the heavenly bodies will control the chemistry of demons in the earth realm until the time of the Messiah's return.

The old King James Version of Joel 3:11 uses the word "Assemble" which means "come to help." The same word form the source of the name Arcturus – ayish which is "oosh." Arcturus the Great Bear and her "sons" in the constellation has always been associated with a Messianic ordinance and ministry. It hides behind the other constellations to help or influence them to align.

The mysteries in the heavenly places will be provoked by the cry of the Saints – the Holy Ones, to move against the astral influences that control the sons of wickedness or the offsprings of Ashtaroth. They will control the weather and influence seasons and what they bring to the earth. Arcturus and his sons are forces of Heaven and part of the armies of God in the heavenly places that will counteract and bring balance to our battle. But they will only respond to the cry of the Saints. Job 38:31-35 says,

> *"Canst thou bind the sweet influences of Pleiades, or loose the bands of Orion? Canst thou bring forth Mazzaroth in his season? Or canst thou guide Arcturus with his sons? Knowest thou the ordinances of heaven? Canst thou set the dominion thereof in the earth? Canst thou lift up thy voice to the clouds, that abundance of waters may cover thee?"*

Every word in the above Bible verses has a coded message for the Church. The Great Bear will bring his bullishness on the sons of the giant on the day of battle. The sons of the Bear will bully the sons of the giants and send them to the valley of Jehoshaphat, where they shall judge them of their wickedness. The Bible says,

> "*Watch ye therefore, and pray always, that ye may be accounted worthy to escape all these things that shall come to pass, and to stand before the Son of man*" (Luke 21:36).

The Watchman and the Saints that will sigh and cry must reach out to the powers of this Great Bear and his sons in the heavenly places IN THE NAME OF JESUS to influence the Zodiac against every strange spirit. The bullish nature of the sons of the giants must be stopped by unleashing the provisions of Heaven to checkmate them through prayer and by the practical action of the Saints to create physical systems in their communities. The Church must be practical and spiritual at the same time to confront and overcome the giants or Ashtaroth and Antichrist.

16

GREAT KINGDOMS, GREAT RIVERS

G reat kingdoms are always associated with great rivers. Babylon had "Chebar", Euphrates and Tigris; Egypt had the Nile, the Mongols had the Mongolian River. The rivers are as great as their nations. The nations get their strength, gods, and inspirations from the river which is their source of life. To conquer them, you have to conquer their rivers. For Babylon to fall, Jeremiah kept on attacking their rivers. Even the great Christian city of Constantinople could not fall until her great river and water supplies were conquered by the armies of Mehmet in 1453. The Bible says;

> *"And there are three that bear witness*
> *in earth, the spirit, and the water, and*
> *the blood: and these three agree in one"*
> (1 John 5:8).

This secret is still applicable today. Before we can rule great nations and empires, we must first conquer their rivers. Make the source of their rivers a prayer point before entering to rule the people.

By prophetic prayer, we control the directions, destinies, politics, governments, and religion of nations.

The Jews in Babylon showed us that secret by always withdrawing to the river banks to pray whenever they face great persecution. There they sang and worshiped Yahweh and cried out day and night for their redemption.

> *"By the rivers of Babylon, there we*
> *sat down, yea, we wept, when we*
> *remembered Zion"* (Psalm 137:1).

Jews in captivity got refuge by the rivers of their captors because, in God's uncanny way, they knew that the lives and destinies of the captors were attached to that river. Daniel, speaking of the power of the river, said:

> *"I ate no pleasant bread, neither came*
> *flesh nor wine in my mouth, neither*

did I anoint myself at all, till three whole weeks were fulfilled. And in the four and twentieth day of the first month, as I was by the side of the great river, which is Hiddekel" (Daniel 10:3-4).

Ezekiel 1:1 says:

"Now it came to pass in the thirtieth year, in the fourth month, in the fifth day of the month, as I was among the captives by the river of Chebar, that the heavens were opened, and I saw visions of God."

"Then I arose, and went forth into the plain: and, behold, the glory of the LORD *stood there, as the glory which I saw by the river of Chebar: and I fell on my face...And the cherubims were lifted up. This is the living creature that I saw by the river of Chebar... And it was according to the appearance of the vision which I saw, even according to the vision that I saw when I came to destroy the city: and the visions were like the vision that I saw by the river Chebar; and I fell upon my face"* (Ezekiel 3:23; 10:15; 43:3).

Seeds of prayers and prophetic travail were made in rivers by Prophets Daniel and Ezekiel until Jehovah showed up for them.

PROPHETIC ACTIONS BY THE RIVER

To save Moses' life, the mother hid him in the river that gave Egypt life – the River Nile. She even named him– "Fetched out of the water." It took a seed of God succored by their river to deliver Israel from Egypt.

Jeremiah gave Prince Seraiah stones riddled with scriptures tied to them to throw into the River Babylon to ensure the return of Israel from captivity after seventy years.

Watchmen should pay special attention to the rivers in the great empires that rule over the nations of the earth if they must establish God's divine dominions and direction over those nations. Great Britain with all her witchcraft and goodness is ruled by River Thames. The watchmen in the land of Britain must establish a special prophetic affiliation to that river to take control, check and rule the destiny of the people in the will of God.

The watchmen of America should pray and disarm the goddess of the great Mississippi River; Kenyans must watch over the Tana River, River Nyansa, River Athi, Mara River, and the Nzoia River.

Zambians should intercede and praise in the Zambezi River, Kafue River, Luapula River, and Luangwa River. Watch out for the "small bone" – Kafue.

Southern African watchmen should take control of the Limpopo and Orange Rivers. Watch out for these rivers that point the directions of the nation. Read their histories and what they were used for and follow the direction or ministration you get to prayer and carry out prophetic actions. Speak to the souls of the people and that nation shall be free. Let the Holy Spirit go into the river to heal the land. Let the prayer of supplications and thanksgiving be made to the Lord of Heaven.

River "Nyanza" or "Nyansa" must be healed and cleansed for Kenyans to be set free. Kafue River in Zambia holds her key. The Nile is the place of the dead; Leviathan must be cut-off – the serpent of Africa.

The water in Liverpool known as Liverpool Bay holds more secrets that affect Great Britain and the region than meets the eye. There is a battle between a raging spirit in the North Sea using the Irish Sea to tame or control the River Thames which the Lord refers to as the Golden River. Liverpool holds the secret of both.

India and Pakistan share a river that holds the umbilical cord of their covenant and troubles. The nerve must be cut-off.

The Mongolian spirit in Asia is still alive and controlling like a covering cherub. Most of the complex spiritual blood covenants by which Mongolia was ruled at its height still control most of Asia. The influences from Asia gave birth to the spirit of the Bulldog in Russia. The Bulldog spirit in Russia can become the powerhouse of God or the chimney of hell.

Nations will need to look inwards to extract themselves from the strange covenants that influence their actions.

> *"And he will destroy in this mountain the face of the covering cast over all people, and the veil that is spread over all nations. He will swallow up death in victory; and the Lord* GOD *will wipe away tears from off all faces; and the rebuke of his people shall he take away from off all the earth: for the* LORD *hath spoken it"* (Isaiah 25:7-8).

That Spirit of the Lord that met Ezekiel by the River Chebar followed him to the mainland in Chapter three verse twenty-three. The glory he contacted by the river while praying over Babylon and the desolation of Israel also followed him to the mainland in Ezekiel 43:3.

The cherubim in Ezekiel 43:3 destroyed the city!

> *"And it was according to the appearance of the vision which I saw, even according to the vision that I saw when I came to destroy the city: and the visions were like the vision that I saw by the river Chebar; and I fell upon my face."*

If Ezekiel had not opened the portal by the river of the city, the great miracle would not have taken place.

In the second sample, in 1 Kings 1:7-53, Adonijah sacrificed sheep, oxen, and fat cattle on a serpent stone of Zoheleth facing a fountain (En-rogel) which was supposed to be the eye of the land (H5869 – Strong Concordance).

> *"And Adonijah slew sheep and oxen and fat cattle by the stone of Zoheleth, which is by En-rogel, and called all his brethren the king's sons, and all the men of Judah the king's servants:"*
> *(1 Kings 1:9)*

Despite that, the hand of the Lord cut him down. So does the Lord to the rivers in nations at the mouth of a prophet or priest or holy men who carry God in their mouths as in the case of "Zadok the priest, and Benaiah the son of Jehoiada, and Nathan the prophet, Shimei and Rei, and the mighty men which belonged to David."

> *"But Zadok the priest, and Benaiah the son of Jehoiada, and Nathan the prophet, and Shimei, and Rei, and the mighty men which belonged to David, were not with Adonijah." (1 Kings 1:8)*

The river spirits with territorial influence were going to be used to carry out a coup against the Messiah and God's plan for Israel through Adonijah and his sacrifice, but Jehovah through other men (Watchmen) scuttled it - 1 Kings 1:7-53. Adonijah was going to use a river spirit to take the crown!

Adonijah used a priest, prophet, and men of war to war against God's will, by a fountain. David used a priest, prophet, and men of war to scuttle them.

All rivers carry a level of divinity and authority.

> *"Art thou better than populous No, that was situate among the rivers, that had the waters round about it,*

whose rampart was the sea, and her
wall was from the sea?" (Nahum 3:8)

To prove that the souls of the nations are attached to the souls of their rivers God said:

"Behold, therefore I am against thee,
and against thy rivers, and I will
make the land of Egypt utterly waste
and desolate, from the tower of Syene
even unto the border of Ethiopia."
(Ezekiel 29:10)

It took this to defeat Egypt. Note Pharaoh's dream in Genesis 41:1-36, 47:18-19. It took the blessings or leanness of the sea to determine the blessing or leanness of the land. Note how the destiny of Egypt became connected to what came out of the sea. Note especially how that the rightful interpretation by Joseph determined the destiny of Egypt and the world of their time.

The genuine Josephs (Issachar Watchmen) of our time will decide how things eventually play out.

"And there are three that bear witness
in earth, the spirit, and the water, and
the blood: and these three agree in
one." (1 John 5:8)

Note, water is always a witness of God on earth. Adonijah invoked the spirit and blood of animals by a fountain water witness and failed. So shall they fail in your nation in Jesus' Name!

> *"And he went forth unto the spring of the waters, and cast the salt in there, and said, Thus saith the LORD, I have healed these waters; there shall not be from thence any more death or barren land. So the waters were healed unto this day, according to the saying of Elisha which he spake." (2 Kings 2:21-22)*

The prophet poured salt into the river to heal the unpleasantness caused by territorial spirits in the land.

All Watchmen must go to river banks to cry out to God for the salvation of the people and cities.

SUNK SHIP RISE IN MONTSERRAT

Dredging of the waterways that formed the entry point for ships into the Island of Montserrat had proved difficult for many years because of a ship that sank since around the 18th Century. Visitors coming by sea had to stop somewhere outside and ferried by boats into the Island.

This affected the economic and commercial prosperity of Montserrat. During our first memorable visit to the Caribbean at the instance of Ambassador Lauren Fenton, the Lord commanded us to do a prophetic prayer walk around the Island that ended at the seaside. There the Lord commanded us to break bread and anoint the waters.

While anointing the waters, a great cloud gathered in the horizon above us, the waters we anointed changed and took a rainbow color from where we anointed it and began to spread before our eyes into the sea in the direction where the sank ship was.

Suddenly the rain began. It rained for seven days and at the end of the seven days, the sunk ship floated. They had spent so much in the past with aid from Great Britain to dredge and remove that ship and did not succeed but the Spirit of the Lord went in the Power of His underwater winds at no price and moved it out.

The local tabloid or was it a British newspaper reported it. They also in the previous years had had a volcanic eruption that consumed half of the Island and drought was threatening. This seven-day rain was a cleanser and saving grace. God had prophetically told us to expect a seven days miracle. Hallelujah!

GUINEA CONAKRY

Artificial Grove by the Source of the River Niger (Guinea Conakry) where Nigeria got its name.

The Priest whose father is called "Diablo." Their family has served the River source as its priest for generations. The first Prime Minister of Nigeria, Sir Abubakar Tafawa Balewa, was reported to have been bathed by the Diablo before he assumed office as Nigeria's Prime Minister according to the narration the current priest gave the team from Throneroom.

SPRING (SOURCE) OF RIVER NIGER

The Prophetic Prayer Commando Team Throneroom sent brought these pictures from the source of the Niger in Guinea Conakry – Pastor Ayuba Bature, Dr. David UdoUmo and Pastor Anayo Dike.

17

THE TREE OF LIFE

Watchmen and the elect of God must eat of the tree of life continually to give life to the people and nation. The flesh of Christ given to all believers is the Word (Matthew 4:4; Ezekiel 3:17; Jeremiah 5:14; Psalm 33:6; Deuteronomy 8:3, 1 Corinthians 10:3-5, John 1:14, John 6:53, Revelations 22:1-4 & 14).

> *"And Balaam said unto Balak, Lo, I am come unto thee: have I now any power at all to say anything? the word that God putteth in my mouth, that shall I speak...And the Lord put a word in Balaam's mouth, and said,*

Return unto Balak, and thus thou shalt speak" (Numbers 22:38; 23:5).

"He that hath an ear, let him hear what the Spirit saith unto the churches; To him that overcometh will I give to eat of the tree of life, which is in the midst of the paradise of God...Blessed are they that do his commandments, that they may have right to the tree of life, and may enter in through the gates into the city" (Revelation 2:7; 22:14).

EAT THE WORD

What you eat is what you will speak. It is what you eat that makes you a "God" – Psalm 82:6. Eat God, be God. Eat the Word, digest it and the life in it shall be released into your spirit. The spirit of God shall enter into whatsoever you speak to. You must eat and drink of HIM to have life and by extension, heal the nations.

John 6:53 says,

"Then Jesus said unto them, Verily, verily, I say unto you, Except ye eat the flesh of the Son of man, and drink his blood, ye have no life in you."

Just as you eat and the food is digested and broken down, and the nutrient is retained to give the body life but what is not needed is discharged as waste, so is the Word of God. Each time you read and digest the word, it is broken down in your thought real but what the Holy Spirit needs you to learn He keeps it circulating within you until it becomes an inspiration, exhortation, instruction, and command to you, and fill every void.

Revelation 22 says that in these last days, the major primordial ministry of the Word will bring healing to the spirit, soul, and flesh. Its second ministry is to wipe away tears and spiritual and physical hunger. The tree will provide fruit for food for the soul, spirit, and body. Leaves (herbs) for the healing of the spirit, soul, and body. Just as it was meant to be in the beginning in Genesis.

Revelation 22:7 gives believers in Christ the right to eat of the tree of life in paradise. Jesus is that tree who is sitting at the right hand of God. He gives those who have washed their garments the right to eat the Word and bring healing to the

world. They are the channel through which the earth receives her healing.

ACTION POINT

1. Wash your garments by **Consecrating**
2. **Yourself.**

3. Go in between the altar and eat the fire of the **Word** (Ezra 10:2).

4. Spread the Word into the city for the **healing** of the nations.

5. Go back to the potter always to remold you.

6. Sow seeds and preach in season and out of season till the fire within you becomes a furnace that you cannot contain.

7. Speak only what God says, even when you do not grasp the meaning and situation completely.

8. Have self-control through the Holy Spirit.

9. Eat the Holy Sacrament from time to time. Every elect and watchman must make it a habit to eat of His broken flesh and drink of His Blood from time to time as an enactment of His covenant and GRACE.

EATING THE FLESH OF JESUS

> *"For my flesh is meat indeed, and my blood is drink indeed. He that eateth my flesh, and drinketh my blood, dwelleth in me, and I in him"* (John 6:55-57). Watchmen should abide in the tree of life if they want to enjoy the presence of Jesus in them.

What happens when Watchmen lives by the Tree of Life – Jesus.

> *"And he shewed me a pure river of water of life, clear as crystal, proceeding out of the throne of God and of the Lamb. In the midst of the street of it, and on either side of the river, was there the tree of life, which bare twelve manner of fruits, and yielded her fruit every month: and the leaves of the tree were for the healing of the nations. And there shall be no more curse: but the throne of God and of the Lamb shall be in it; and his servants shall serve him: And they shall see his face; and his name shall be in their foreheads. And there shall be no night there; and they need no candle, neither light of the sun; for the Lord God giveth them light: and they shall reign forever and ever"*
> (Revelation 22:1-5).

The Tree of Life automatically changes the life of watchmen who stay closer to Jesus.

REWARDS OF WATCHMEN WHO LIVE BY THE TREE OF LIFE

1. They live long. Examples are Anna, Simeon, and John.
2. They enjoy times and seasons of refreshing (Acts 3).
3. They are ruled by a Kingdom government, that Jesus is the King.
4. They are renewed daily.
5. They are more than conquerors. Witchcraft, sorcery, and curses cannot affect their activities.
6. They have immunity over the plagues that afflict the world (Acts 12:1, 23).
7. They are made to be like the Angels of Heaven.
8. They are ruled by the laws and gravity of Christ; whatever cannot happen to Christ cannot happen to them.
9. They are empowered to defeat Satan and his agents. God will always make a way of escape for them on earth.

VISION OF THE SON AND THE TREE OF LIFE

In the vision of the king of Babylon when he went out to check out the three Hebrew boys he threw into the furnace, he saw a fourth man like the Son of God amongst them (Daniel 3:25).

The presence of Jesus stopped the furnace from consuming the three men. Acts Chapter 7:38, 4445 says Jesus is the One who went with them in the wilderness and brought the blessings of grace so that they were not consumed by their sins and the laws of Moses.

He was the gift of life that stopped the wilderness from devouring Israel. He was their great deliverance and towering fire above them in the wilderness. You need the vision of Christ to survive the seasons of great tribulation and persecution by the Antichrist.

The Tree of Life never left them alone but saved them and wiped away their tears. He did not allow the "son of affliction" to afflict them unto spiritual death. You should always long for the presence of the Son of God because when He is with you, you will not be afraid or be moved by anything.

Psalm 16:8 says,

> "I have set the LORD always before me: because he is at my right hand, I shall not be moved."

Acts 2:25 also says,

> "For David speaketh concerning him, I foresaw the Lord always before my

face, for he is on my right hand, that I should not be moved."

When the Tree of Life is in your midst, nothing can decide your fate except Him. He decides the mercy that comes to you and the judgment. The Lord in the midst of us is mighty. Allow Him to stand in the midst of you always. Offer to Him a sacrifice that will please Him. Let Him be God in your life and family. A personal revelation of Him always precedes His glorious manifestations.

The Tree of Life according to Revelation 22 had twelve fruits, representing the twelve tribes of Israel and the twelve disciples. The disciples are the foundation of the Church and the fulfillment of the promise to Abraham. The twelve fruits are from the Tree of Life. Our fruitfulness comes from the Son of God – Jesus, our Saviour. Make Him sit in the center of your life. The Apokalupsis of Jesus will rule all things in the last days.

> *"I saw in the night visions, and, behold, one like the Son of man came with the clouds of heaven and came to the Ancient of days, and they brought him near before him. And there was given him dominion, and glory, and a kingdom, that all people, nations, and languages, should serve him: his dominion is an everlasting dominion, which shall not pass away,*

and his kingdom that which shall not
be destroyed" (Daniel 7:13-15).

What you see is what rules your domain. Cry unto God for the revelation of the Son of Man to rule your domain. Invite Him to take total charge over your life and all that concerns you. He has to rewrite your visions to be according to His program and plan for you before He can rule in your domain.

TESTIMONIES & PICTORIALS

**SOME OF THE WRITTEN TESTIMONIES & PICTORIALS
SENT IN FROM VARIOUS PARTS OF NIGERIA**

Prophet Emmanuel Kure praying for the nation (Nigeria)
with President Goodluck Jonathan (first from left) and
some leaders at a breakfast meeting.

Apostle Chuck Pierce, President Goodluck Jonathan, Apostle
Dr. Emmanuel Nuhu Kure in Aso Villa, Abuja – Nigeria

The last four clergymen to see late President Umaru
YarAdua alive. Prof. Yusuf Obaje, Bishop David Oyedepo,
Apostle Dr. Emmanuel Kure, and Archbishop John
Onaiyekan

Apostle Emmanuel Kure with Nigerian Speaker, House of Rep – Hon Yakubu Dogara at the 9th National Prayer Breakfast – National Assembly Parliamentary Fellowship Group, Abuja – Nigeria – November 2018

Mr. Boss Mustapha, Secretary to the Nigerian Prophet Emmanuel Kure prophesying to Mr. Boss Government in a warm handshake with Apostle Kure. Mustapha – Secretary to the Nigerian Government.

Apostle Dr. Kure praying for the Speaker, House of Rep –
Hon. Yakubu Dogara and Secretary to Nigerian
Government – Mr. Boss Mustapha

Prophet Kure anointing and praying for members of the
Nigerian House of Representatives and Senate during
the 9th National Prayer Breakfast – National Assembly
Parliamentary Fellowship Group, Abuja – Nigeria –
November 2018

OLU OF WARRI, HIS MAJESTY, OGIAME ATUWATSE II, GODWIN TORITSEJU EMIKO

I was preaching in Warri city in Nigeria for three
days to finish Saturday and leave Sunday. In
those days between the 1990s to 2000s I
preached a lot with the Full Gospel Businessmen
Fellowship International and in some of the local

churches. The first night after the night's program I got emissaries from the palace that the Olu (king) was ill and they were asked to bring me that night. I had a close relationship with the Olu and his wife from when they were in Lagos.

They use to attend weekend special prayer programs as a preacher at the then Engineering Close Parish of the Redeemed Christian Church of God under Pastor Adetola in Victoria Island, Lagos. They single-handedly roofed our first administrative block at our International Headquarters in Kafanchan. I had always paid my respects each time I was in town.

That night, I was told the Olu was ill and would want me to come to pray with him. I asked them to allow me to seek God's face that night and would come in the morning. That was my saving grace because as I sought God's face throughout the night, the Spirit of the Lord would not let me sleep but showed me four spirits and a dug grave beside the Olu's naked body. And the spirits were administering strange ointments on his body preparing him for burial. He seemed to be trapped in a spell.

The Lord said the solution laid at the shrine of his ancestors. Otherwise, he would die, and that I had to step into that shrine and cut off the sorcery by which his soul was trapped and neutralize the death spell. Otherwise, he would die within seven days. The Lord showed that I had to go by water in a boat of my choice with two elders to stand with me in a spiritual governmental agreement.

The next day I met the king at his upstairs living private sitting room where his second throne is situated. He came in after I was seated, sat on the throne, and would not talk. For an embarrassing fifteen minutes, nobody was talking. He just fixed his gaze on me and kept quiet. His huge regal frame gazing at me made me very uncomfortable as it looked like he was making a rethink whether to speak or not. I asked him what the matter was. No answer.

The Lord at that point told me to tell him what I saw the previous night. That opened his mouth as it also contained the solution. He was amazed that I saw everything happening to him as he said he didn't know how to explain it to my understanding since I was not from their tradition and would not understand.

He explained how at night four so-called ancestral spirits would visit him and bath him and oil him up. Each of them had the head of different animals on human bodies and hands and will oil him up with a dug grave waiting for the seventh day when they would put him into the grave. He had completed the third day of those rituals with his state of health with each passing day. He was dying slowly.

He told me how he had gone three days earlier to hold court in his palace official throne and found all kinds of rituals spilled all over the throne. Strangled bird stuffed with all kinds of voodoo stuff in them and the feathers with blood spots scattered on his throne. It symbolized traditionally that he had been spiritually dethroned by force and was meant to join his ancestors (die) in seven days. Sighting it activates it in the body of the king. From that day he took ill and the ritual of those spirits appearing every night to oil him to prepare him for death began. The tradition is that if during those seven days, his wife or anyone else should see him they would die with him. They communicated with his wife with the door dividing them.

They agreed to send for me knowing I was a stranger from another culture and a high priest of God who had dealt with these issues before and who is a friend of the family. They did not know I was in town. So, it was "coincidence" that the emissaries were to come to Kafanchan only to find that I arrived Warri that day for a program. The handbills were everywhere.

I told him what the instruction God gave me in the night without which he would not be delivered. That I needed to go to the ancient shrine of his ancestors to destroy its powers over his life through his ancestors and the covenant tied to his throne. He offered his royal boat to take me for safety and I insisted God would not let me. He now gave me one of his most trusted Christian elders in the kingdom – Dr. Mark Oghaverumi to go with me. I invited another senior Christian leader who worked as a Director in Halliburton and was president of Shalom Ministries – Dr. Eric Omebuani to join us.

The trip to Itsekiri Ode the next day being the fourth day of the king's "sickness" by sea was uneventful. But the return was almost impossible. Mid-way into our return the sea rose with an underwater current that threatened to capsize the canoe. The canoe engine suddenly went off with the waves shoving us everywhere. People at the shore began to scream. The canoe driver had to ask us like in the Biblical Jonah case what we had done and what kind of people we were that the gods were after us. And with that, he jumped into the sea and swam the distance to the shore. I couldn't swim. I still cannot swim.

There was panic on the boat with waves rising and falling and trying to capsize the boat. While contemplating what to do, I heard the Lord say to me "hold your peace and see the salvation of the Lord." I immediately had an audible voice in my spirit command me to put my hands into the sea and prophesy Nahum chapter two verse six and command the palaces of Satan in the sea to be dissolved and be destroyed.

He asked me to rebuke the spirit of Leviathan and command the waves to stop. All the others were screaming in tongues loudly and agreeing with me with big "Amens!" Suddenly, the sea was calm. There were screams of joy on the shore. God sent another boat to bring us the fuel for our engine and took us to shore safely. What did we do to get Satan to make the sea want to consume us?

We had worshipped the Lord at the palace gates and prophesied to the first shrine that was to the left immediately you enter the palace gates in Itsekiri Ode, and commanded the shrine to let the king go and serve the purpose for which he was born and sent by the Owner of the heavens and the earth – the Lord JEHOVAH.

We proceeded from there to the main shrine where the kings take their oaths to Satan. The famous historical shrine from which their kings were reputed to have sent bees to sting the invading bands of colonialists in the days of the scramble for Africa. A small tribe that could not be conquered, the Europeans had to make peace with their kings because of the mysteries of their kings which was reputed to come from this historical famous altar. The chief high priest of the Itsekiri people was reputed to go there only once a year to offer sacrifice for the people like the Biblical Jewish Chief High priest did. The only other time it was approached was when the

Itsekiri nation was at war with formidable enemies.

If I had not heard God clearly in that vision the two nights before, I would not have gone. This shrine is not your ordinary kind of shrine. We had to follow some kind of bush path within the palace to reach it. It is at the other end of the palace and it extends or flows into the sea from the ground. It looked like an ancient grove with an ancient tree at the end of the grove that is partly on the ground and partly in the sea with a deep hole at the root of the tree that enters with the roots into the waters.

A few meters before reaching the shrine, the two elders with me refused to go any further. They suddenly began to feel like the blood in their veins was being dried up or emptied and they were only standing on their bones. We all were speaking in tongues as we approached the ancient famous grove not knowing what to expect except that the attacks had begun. From that moment, they told me I was on my own since I was the one that heard the Lord say directly to come, and was the one originally sent. Before I could answer them, they began to speak in tongues to release me for the final lap.

They were right, I was the one that God sent, and for me, it was a test as to whether the vision I saw was real and whether my God was true. We held hands and prayed to ask for strength to be restored to their bodies. I then proceeded to approach the entry point of the shrine which was built with raffias at the front and surrounded all groves with different tree growths and branches.

As I stepped in pleading the blood of Jesus I was temporarily blinded by the darkness inside. But as my eyes began to adjust to the darkness, I saw some really big eggs (I don't know to which animal they belong) with something like blood sprayed on top of them I also saw calabashes with all sorts of things in them I couldn't tell because there was not enough light.

Then I heard a movement and I froze. I was busy trying to take in the environment inside that I didn't see the big python snake which had risen to its height in the grove and was restlessly hovering over me hissing and moving from one side to the other while the rest of its body was on top of those eggs and the tail extending to the huge hole in the tree. I froze and for a second I was lost, my throat was dry and fear had overtaken me.

Then I heard the Spirit of God remind me that I was only a messenger and should speak like one. Even if I wanted to run, my legs would not carry me. I mustered courage and obeyed the Voice I heard and in stammering, I spoke not sure whether I could hear my voice and addressed the snake that I had no beef (problem) with it but the ONE whom I served had commanded me to tell the shrine and them that dwelt in it in the name of Jesus to let the king go.

I did not know where I got the courage to reach out to the salt and anointing oil I had carried with me and threw the salt of covenant on the eggs and began to command the spell on the king and the land broken. I did not have the grace to look at the snake but concentrated on the eggs on which it stood pouring both the salt and olive anointing oil and commanding them and their powers to be destroyed in the name of Jesus.

Then I heard a loud, shrill cry from the snake and it began to hit the grove from one end to the other. I quickly poured the remaining oil on the calabashes ordering and commanding a release in the name of Jesus and ran out expecting to be bitten or swallowed. I noticed as I ran that the snake was struggling to bring out the rest of its trunk from the trunk hole of the ancient tree whose trunk roots were partly in the waters.

Outside I poured the remaining sea salt on the raffias that formed the door since the Lord had commanded me not to return with any salt and called the Lord to arise and smite the lintel of the door according to Amos chapter nine verse one to four.

I met the others already calling out my name as they were not sure what had happened to me inside as they heard sounds and I was taking too long. I don't know what happened to the snake or the shrine after we left. But we returned to the palace after the sea experience.

On our return, we found the king completely whole. He had suddenly felt things falling off his body while I was having that fight. We found him bathed and fully dressed in his kingly regalia waiting on the upstairs throne. He had feared for our lives and ordered that people should pray for us. I took him to his main throne in the palace and prayed over the throne, removed all the rituals and sacrifices that were made on it, anointed, and rededicated the throne. And asked him to sit for the Lord had told me to re-consecrate him king again. It will be His spiritual seal on the throne.

I made him sit on the throne, anointed him, and ordained him God's king over the land. I anointed his crown and prayed for him, and stepped down from the aisle of the throne and paid obeisance to him as the Lord's king exactly as the Lord had commanded me. With this, my mission was accomplished. I traveled back on Sunday only to be told that the chief high priest had gathered the remaining chiefs and started the traditional dirge for a dead king. As they came into the palace, they found the king on the throne. The chief high priest was exiled out of the land thereafter. This is one of the greatest experiences of God in my life.

Prophet Emmanuel Nuhu Kure with the Olu of Warri,
Ogiame Atuwatse II, Chief Godwin Toritseju Emiko

Atuwatse II was one of the most fearless,
intelligent, and wise Royal Fathers I ever met.
Always had a tangible and wise thing to say.
Very, very passionate about his people. He
yearned to see his people put on the world map
but the many tribulations he had to go through
because of his faith in Christ in a world and
society that will rather have tradition rule over
them than Christ. I remember I had to dodge
bullets in a convoy with soldiers given me by His
Excellency, the then governor of Imo State
Colonel P. K. Zubairu, to go see the Olu. The
roads were not safe and I insisted ongoing.

I was accompanied to the palace by a former shell paymaster and Full Gospel Businessmen Fellowship International leader, Felix Omofuma. The Olu had called me while I was visiting the governor with a mind to pass to Warri to pray with the king because of the crisis with the neighboring tribes had gotten to open hostilities to the extent that the king's palace and tribe were surrounded and being attacked by warring factions from another tribe. He was seriously worried about his people. So, I told him I would keep my promise as he had become isolated in the palace.

I didn't know how serious it was until my convoy of security personnel and I came under a volley of bullets on all sides while we were on the last lap of our trip into the gates of his palace. Our soldiers had to fire back until we entered the gates of the palace. To my utter shock, the Olu had no security men guarding the palace, only the gatekeeper and the angels of heaven. His faithful, doting wife was to join him later. Otherwise, how would you explain how he survived days of siege around the palace with bullets flying everywhere.

We found him in high spirits stubbornly holding on to his faith that his Father in heaven would never leave him. I will never forget the impact that had on me. He told us that he chose to stay with his people rather than hide, and released everyone else in the palace to take refuge. I wonder who will someday tell these stories of a brave king.

I pray God gives us kings and leaders like him. We prayed with him, anointed him, had fellowship with him, and took another way out of Warri, and despite that we still had a few bullets shot at us. The soldiers in my car at one point had to make me lie flat on my seat while they and the two other escort vehicles returned fire. God took us back to Owerri safely. These are memories that bring emotions to me each time I think of them. To God be the glory.

I salute a great first-class king who fought many battles to see that the glory of his small but glorious tribe exalted as his forefathers did. A king who kept faith with God and defended the testimony of our Lord Jesus Christ daily. A king who established a Foursquare Gospel Church branch in his palace instead of a shrine and was involved in missions.

To Olu Ogiame Atuwatse II Chief Godwin Toritseju Emiko, who has gone home to be with the Lord. Rest in peace great son of God. Rest beloveth!

Dr. Kure.

BAYELSA

EXPLOITS IN BAYELSA STATE, NIGERIA
– Written by Prof. O. M. O. Etebu

Bayelsa State is in the South-South geo-political zone of Nigeria and Yenagoa is her capital city. In the year 2003, Throneroom (Trust) Ministry, in conjunction with the Pentecostal Fellowship of Nigeria – Bayelsa Chapter, organized a statewide evangelical crusade in which Apostle Prophet Dr. Emmanuel Nuhu Kure was the only key minister who delivered the word of God. The program was a huge success in that at the end of it some people were seen lying face down, struck by the Holy Ghost, at the center curb of the dualized road by the Government House, Yenagoa, because the venue of the program was at the sand field contiguous to Creek Haven – the Government House is known as Creek Haven.

Preceding this statewide program was a rally covering the entire Yenagoa city alongside all gateways of the town. As the procession progressed to a roadside community known as Agudama-Epie, along Mbiama-Yenagoa Road, Prophet Kure's attention was called to the existence of a big – thick – evil bush known as Asegberi Juju forbidden forest where no human being, except the worshippers, dared access or enter.

Asegberi juju forbidden forest was owned by Ogbobiri compound in Agudama Epie community in Yenagoa Local Government Area of Bayelsa State, geographically located directly opposite the headquarters of Central Naval Command, Camp Porbeni Yenagoa. A reliable source said that the idol named Asebiri was so terrible that nobody urinated, spat, or defecated in the vicinity of the forest, for the penalty of such act was death.

Sources from the community had it that in the ancient times, in case an indigene broke breakable plates or if valuable things got spoilt or damaged, the owner of the damaged items would drop them in the forest, returned the following day, and collect brand new ones from the forest.

Prophet Kure was briefed of the fact that incessant accidents occurred there and that just about a week before then, an 18-seat bus had a fatal accident by the shrine and that all the occupants of the vehicle had died on the spot. This axis of the road is within the town so it is not as if commuters drive beyond the speed limit. Hence many accidents occurred.

Prophet Kure entered the dreaded forest along with Police Officer, Mohammed Abdullahi, who on sighting the shrine shot at it on impulse and out of fear. In the narrative of Mohammed

Abdullahi, he targeted his gun at a tree which served as a gate/barrier to the shrine and fired just once, and then the gun got jammed and thereafter was no longer serviceable. According to him, he saw a red cloth, white cloth, cooked food (*garri and soup*), calabash, blood, and seats for the worshippers who paid allegiance to the idol.

Since 2003, when Prophet Kure desecrated those strange altars, there have been no accidents at that spot at Agudama Epie because the bloodthirsty shrine could not cause mishaps any longer and therefore lives are no longer lost there. More heartwarming is the fact that the forest has been evacuated and a Church named Branch of Christ Mission International bought, built, and occupied the so-called "forbidden forest" since 2011.

Prophet Emmanuel Kure dedicating and commissioning the Throneroom Tower, Yenagoa with Prof. Ongoebi M. O. Etebu.

During this particular program, the good Lord created also an opportunity for Prophet Kure to commission the Throneroom (Trust) Ministry Tower at Yenagoa and ordained Dr.
Ongoebi Maureen Etebu into her calling.
Presently, Prof. Etebu is the Pioneer Vice Chancellor of the Premier Nigeria Maritime University, Okerenkoko.

OGUTA, IMO STATE

His Royal Highness, Ezeigwe of Oguta blowing a horn during one of the Deliverance Crusade held for 3 years (2010-2013).

Prophet Dr. Emmanuel Nuhu Kure making prophetic declarations over the land at the Oguta Deliverance Crusade, Imo State, Nigeria.

CALABAR, CROSS RIVER

APOSTLE DR EMMANUEL NUHU KURE THE PROPHET OF OUR TIME

Surely the LORD God will do nothing, but he reveals his secret unto his servants the prophet". (Amos 3:7) Papa Emmanuel Kure has been a great spiritual influence on the current move of God in Cross River State and Calabar City in particular in her development. The first major contact he had with the land was in 1999 when he was hosted to the Calabar Prophetic Crusade.

Prophet Kure, the Obong of Calabar, Prof. Elijah Henshaw (arrowed), and Prayer City host, Rev. Theodore Effiong (arrowed) at His Royal Majesty's Palace, Calabar - Nigeria

Apostle Dr. Simon Paul, formerly Dr. Charles Edem was the Chairman of the Central Planning committee while I served as the Head of the Prayer Committee. That meeting became the catalyst to the modern development that the state witnessed.

Prophet Kure ministering to Barr. Kanu Agabi (SAN) the former Minister of Justice & Attorney General of the Federation (Nigeria).

A section of the crowd at the Crusade Ground

In that meeting, the former Governor of the state, Mr. Donald Duke and his government were dedicated to God at the cultural Centre, Calabar. The Governor was represented by his deputy, the late Mr. John Okpa. In the course of the meeting, Papa Kure prophesied about the developments and transformations that were later witnessed in Cross River State under Mr. Donald Duke. I still have the messages of that meeting in which he extensively unveiled what Cross River State was about witnessing.

On the Saturday of that meeting, we undertook a prophetic march on long motor convoys prophesying and anointing with oil the land, along major streets, roundabouts, graveyards, rivers and streams, altars, shrines, public buildings, the popular eleven, eleven, etc,. Prayer City, 7 Marina Road, Calabar was the venue of the program.

The prophetic march covered the four major city gates led by Apostle Kure, Rev. Ugochukwu Okike, Apostle Simon Paul, and Apostle Elias Emmanuel.

The program encompassed the churches in Calabar in collaboration with other Christian bodies like Full Gospel Business Men Fellowship.

Prophetic March to a Major Shrine in the Ancient City of Calabar - Nigeria

Apostle Kure went into Hawkins Cemetery and Marina Beach. He prophesied and anointed them. It was unprecedented spiritual work, and that night heavy rain fell in the land.

Over the years, the prophetic work with Apostle Kure in the land continued with Cross River Prayer Summit. This work was taken a step further with prayer convocation at the Palace of the Obong of Calabar with the then Obong of Calabar, His Majesty Late Ndidem Professor Elijah Henshaw, the tongue talking Holy Ghost filled Obong of Calabar. All these meetings attracted huge crowds cutting across the clergy, laity, business class, political class, academia, and the ordinary people. I can boldly say that each of these meetings had major physical, spiritual, and developmental dimensional shifts.

Destroying Altars at the Obong's Palace. Obong Prof. Elijah Henshaw making Proclamations of Release

God had been using Apostle Kure as a watchman over the land of Cross River State and he has a great burden for the land and was always willing to respond to the cry of the people to come over Macedonia to help us. In other instances, he had come to minister in the land on the invitation of the state government. The government of Mr. Liyel Imoke had also hosted him at the Calabar Stadium. God had been using him to unveil deep mysteries about the land. During the time of Mr. Donald Duke, he organized a high-powered prophetic work from Calabar to Obudu Cattle Ranch.

In recent times, specifically last year, he visited the land at the instance of Chapel of Redemption, University of Calabar, Calabar under the leadership of Rev. Nsa Eyo for a two-day explosive prophetic meeting. This meeting was mind-blowing in which he broke a pot addressing the major seat of wickedness in the land.

God has endowed him with able foot soldiers in executing these assignments in the land, among whom are Apostle Ofodile Nzimiro, the Vision Coordinator of Throneroom Trust Ministry, Kafanchan, Kaduna State of Nigeria, and Apostle PK Ayuba.

I must appreciate some individuals whom God has been using to bring Apostle Kure in the land; Apostle Dr. Simon Paul, Apostle Elias Emmanuel; Rev. Theodore Effiong, Rev. Ephraim Effiong, Rev. Mrs. Gift Effiong, Commander Obanya, Mrs. Rose
Obanya, Hon. Bassey Ibor, Surveyor Aniyom Akamkpo, Mr. Dan Oku, members of Cross River Prayer Summit, and others too numerous to mention.

Apostle Dr. Emmanuel Nuhu Kure is an immense blessing to Cross River State and I know the Lord will still use him to help the land position well for her ordained blessings from God.

Rev. Ugochukwu Nkem Okike (JP)
Senior Pastor, Christian Pentecostal Mission Int.
Calabar, Cross River State.

RIVERS STATE

Apostle Dr. Kure, Governor Nyesom Wike &
Deputy Governor, Mrs. Banigo

Governor Wike, Deputy Gov. Banigo, some his Executives,
and Apostle Kure's team

Apostle Kure with Former Governor,
Timipre Sylva

*Apostle Kure praying for Rivers State & Nigeria
from Govt. House, Port Harcourt – Nigeria.*

Throneroom Tower – Port Harcourt

IBADAN/ILORIN

In 2018 the Lord had instructed Apostle Emmanuel Nuhu Kure to raise a standard in Ibadan to avoid a major traditional civil war or unrest and a breakdown of law and order because a spiritual portal has been opened and key spirits released to war. Sudden mysterious deaths of key traditional institutions and related agencies might take place that will threaten the stability of the rest of the society and in turn, affect the rest of the Yoruba race. A major prophetic prayer cry was raised as instructed by the Lord for the land and the people.

The Olubadan of Ibadanland, Oba Saliu Adetunji joining to pray for the destiny of the Yoruba race and dedicating them back to God.

Apostle Kure's Prophetic visit to the Olubadan of Ibadanland Palace in Oyo State – Nigeria.

The Spirit of the Lord said Ilorin is one of the major sources of the strength and witchcraft of the Fulani herdsmen. He asked that the hideous foundational covenants be broken between the Afonja family and the Fulanis, and demand be made that Nigeria should be released from the venom of the serpent in the spring of water flowing in one of the surrounding suburbs of Ilorin.

Afonja and Alimi Families in Prophetic Praying Prophesying to the Ancients for Change in Ilorin – Kwara State.

Prophet Kure praying at the source of the River in Ilorin – Kwara – Nigeria

This is the report forwarded to Apostle Sir. Gbolahan Olayomi, one of the key Apostles in the ministry. The report:

Several testimonies followed the 2018 edition of the prayer convocation. Some of them are as follows:

1. The Olubadan, an Islamic Monarch, was publicly led to accept the Lord Jesus by Apostle Emmanuel Kure. As at present, he

is more disposed to the Lordship of Jesus than to the Islamic faith.

2. The Olubadan never parted with the prophetic stones he collected during the convocation. He is already agitating to receive Apostle Kure again in his palace in particular and Ibadan in general.

3. Almost all the prophetic pronouncements made during the convocation have come to pass.

4. The wind of change that blew in the political landscape of Oyo State resulting in the electoral victory of Engr. Seyi Makinde as the new governor is not unconnected with the impact of the prayer convocation. The prayer convocations were called to stop the strange winds of dead and great catastrophize that were threatening the state and the whole of the Yoruba race. God said Ibadan was one of the few places where the fate and secret of the Yoruba people laid. That is why He sent Apostle Kure to secure that future.

5. Since the prayer convocation was held the State has witnessed a period of tremendous peace in all areas.

6. Prophetic actions were carried out by the prophetic team that was raised at the close of the convocation within and outside Ibadan. Many spiritual gates and major strongholds were visited.

7. Natural disasters, like floods, that were previously predicted by government agencies to happen in Ibadan were eventually averted.

8. The prophetic counsel of the Lord given by Apostle Kure was the catalyst for resolving the lingering crisis between the Olubadan and his chiefs who had been elevated to obas by the then state governor and had rebelled against his sovereignty in the land. The crisis has now been resolved and the
Olubadan is still sovereign over the land and the chiefs have accepted to serve under him.

9. Oyo State has witnessed exponential economic prosperity since 2018. It has regained its position as the capital of the Yoruba race after the Prophetic Prayer Convocations of 2018 and 2019.

Pa Olusola Ajolore, Prophet Dr. Kure & Evang.
Prof. T. O. Opoola (CAN Chairman, Kwara State.

Ilorin Elders Breaking Bread over the Land.

Pictures of Iwo Road Roundabout, Ibadan during a festive period. Ibadan public places are always empty at night but the people were out on this night celebrating their newfound prosperity.

THRONEROOM

Throneroom Evangelical Jesus Train!

Gen Yakubu Gowon (former Head of State) and other
dignitaries At a Programme in Kafanchan – Nigeria

Bishop David Oyedepo stepping into Zion
International Prayer Retreat Camp, Kafanchan

Passover Meeting at the Zion International Prayer Retreat Camp,
Kafanchan – Kaduna – Nigeria

Dignitaries and conferees from other nations at the Passover
Meeting.

Former Governor Danbaba Suntai (Taraba State)
joining us for Prayers in Kafanchan – Nigeria

Prof. Jerry Gana (former Minister of Information), Sen. Anyim Pius Anyim (former Senate President), Pastor Martha Kure & Apostle Dr. Emmanuel Kure.

Former Gov. Bonni Haruna (Adamawa State) and former Minister for Petroleum, Hon. Diezani Alison-Maduke and other dignitaries attending a conference in Kafanchan.

FATHERS AND MENTORS

Pastor Enoch A. Adeboye

Dr. C. Peter Wagner

Dr. C. Peter Wagner, Apostle Chuck Pierce, and Dr. Pat Francis
ordaining Apostle Kure as the African Ambassador and
Convening Apostle for Africa - Global Spheres International.

SALVATION PRAYER

If you have not invited the Lord Jesus Christ to save your soul and give you eternal life make peace with Him now to make all that is written in this book to be meaningful to you.

> *"Neither is there salvation in any other: for there is none other name under heaven given among men, whereby we must be saved." (Acts 4:12)*

> *"That if thou shalt confess with thy mouth the Lord Jesus, and shalt believe in thine heart that God hath raised him from the dead, thou shalt be saved. 10 For with the heart, man believeth unto righteousness; and with the mouth, confession is made unto salvation." (Romans 10:9-10)*

Kneel now and invite Him to forgive you your sins, reconcile your life with His, and eternally save your soul. Ask Him to enter your heart and rule eternally as Lord and Saviour and instantly, you will be translated in the spirit as one of His, and His peace will come into your heart.

"Who is the image of the invisible God,
the firstborn of every creature:"
(Colossians 1:13)